MY SUNFLOWER GIRL

LOSS, GRIEF AND GLORY

DYFAN WILLIAMS

MUDIAD EFENGYLAIDD CYMRU — EVANGELICAL MOVEMENT OF WALES

To read *My Sunflower Girl* is to overhear the soliloquy of Dyfan Williams, husband, father, and pastor, as he walks through the dark valley where shadows fall around him from the death of his beloved daughter Megan. As in King David's great psalm there is a confession of deep faith ('The Lord is my Shepherd, I shall not want'). But at times these pages also become conversations between a bruised but trusting soul and the Lord whose presence holds him fast in the dark ('you are with me, your rod and staff they comfort me').

Personal loss is profoundly individual. Yet here, in the poetic soul of Dyfan Williams, you will find an honesty combined with faith, an understanding nourished by experience, and a compassionate and gentle pastoral wisdom. *My Sunflower Girl* is a profoundly moving testimony to God's presence with his people in their darkest hours.

— SINCLAIR B FERGUSON, CHANCELLOR'S PROFESSOR OF SYSTEMATIC THEOLOGY AT REFORMED THEOLOGICAL SEMINARY, ASSISTANT MINISTER AT ST. PETER'S FREE CHURCH OF SCOTLAND, DUNDEE

Here is a father's compelling narrative describing the unexpected death of his ten-year-old daughter Megan. The book is well written, factual and honest. Readers may soon find tears in their eyes as they read of the overwhelming grief and pain felt by parents and family in losing their precious daughter. Probing questions are asked in a prayerful and struggling submission to the sovereign providence of God yet in the context of the glory awaiting believers like Megan who trust in Christ. I urge you to read the book and share it with others too.

— Eryl Davies, Elder, Heath Church, Cardiff and Research Supervisor, Union School of Theology

To lose your daughter at the age of ten would leave one reeling with grief and crying out in anguish to God. The loss of Megan and the impact on Dyfan, his wife Caroline and their children Lloyd and Siân is deep, distressing and lasting but you will see God's presence and faithfulness evident through the darkest of days.

Dyfan writes in a calm and disarmingly honest way, recalling Megan's death as if it were very recent and yet the perspective that time gives is beneficial. To have such a book written by a father provides an important perspective. Dyfan's thoughtful reflections on Scripture and sensitive use of poetry ensure the pain of death and the parting that results are not minimised and yet he shows how strength, comfort and help were provided. The insight Dyfan gives into such deep grief will resonate with all who suffer but also provide understanding and sensitivity to those who walk alongside. He doesn't evade the heartfelt cry "Why?"

I would encourage you to read this book and be helped. You will not forget Megan, her loss and the Williams family, but it will also strengthen your hold on the one who is always with us; never leaves us or forsakes us and never lets us go. As your feet remain here on earth the eyes of your heart will be lifted towards heaven.

— ELINOR MAGOWAN, WOMEN'S MINISTRY CO-ORDINATOR FIEC AND PASTOR'S WIFE, CAREY BAPTIST CHURCH READING

What a moving book! Dyfan honestly, delicately, wisely, and faithfully lets us into his experience of losing his beloved daughter Megan when she was only ten years old. As he so helpfully tells this story, the Lord through him can minister to our own heartache, bewilderment, and sorrow. There are no simple answers, or fairy tale endings here. The confusion, pain, anger, and lasting sense of loss are all described in ways that others who have gone through dark valleys will recognise. But the comfort of the gospel is brought to bear, and "the solid joy and lasting treasure" of the Christian good news shines brightly out into our dark and needy world. Highly commended.

— Ray Evans, Senior Pastor, Grace Community Church, Bedford, FIEC Church Leadership Consultant

The death of a child must be one of the most devastating and painful experiences we can know. In this beautifully written but brutally honest book, Dyfan Williams describes the life-changing effects on the whole family of the death of his daughter, Megan, at only ten years old. The short chapters are easy to read but avoid any pat answers. Instead you are invited to share in the sacred and sad journey of parents called to walk through the darkness of the valley of death. The interweaving of quotations from poetry and Scripture offer a positive counterpoint to the painful narrative of Megan's passing. There are no easy answers here but there is hope, as faith, though stretched almost to breaking point in a loving God, is finally the basis on which the reality of life without their Sunflower girl can begin to be rebuilt. In the preface the author expresses his hope that God "will use the book to bring help to those who may be called to walk through similar dark valleys; to those who are called to offer comfort by walking with them; and to those who would like to know more about the hope that can be found through Jesus Christ." I am happy to say he succeeds in all three objectives.

— PHIL JENKINS, MINISTER OF ST. ANDREWS
INTERNATIONAL CHURCH, ATHENS

ISBN 978-1-78397-259-3

The Evangelical Movement of Wales works in both Welsh and English and seeks to help Christians and churches by:

• running children's camps and family conferences

• providing theological training and events for ministers

• running Christian bookshops and a conference centre

• publishing magazines and books.

Bryntirion Press is a ministry of EMW. Past issues of EMW magazines and sermons preached at our conferences are available on our website: www.emw.org.uk

Published by Bryntirion Press, Waterton Cross Business Park, South Road, Bridgend CF31 3UL, in association with:

EP Books (Evangelical Press), Registered Office: 140 Coniscliffe Road, Darlington, Co Durham DL3 7RT

admin@epbooks.org www.epbooks.org

EP Books in the USA are distributed by:

JPL Books, 3883 Linden Ave. S.E., Wyoming, MI 49548

order@jplbooks.com www.jplbooks.com

To Caroline, Lloyd and Siân
Ringrazio Dio per ciascuno di voi.
Quanto mi siete cari!

Ah, Sun-flower! weary of time,
Who countest the steps of the Sun:
Seeking after that sweet golden clime
Where the traveller's journey is done;

Where the Youth pined away with
  desire,
And the pale Virgin shrouded in snow,
Arise from their graves and aspire,
Where my Sun-flower wishes to go.

William Blake

CONTENTS

FOREWORD

Every once in a while, I read something that draws me in —heart and mind—and manages to speak to the depths of my being. This stunning and poignant memoir did precisely that. Dyfan and I had been colleagues together in UCCF during the 90s and he subsequently heard about the death of my sister's eleven year- old son and decided to send me an early draft of *My Sunflower Girl* to see if I had any constructive comments on the text.

I settled down at my desk to read it in a work-man like and objective frame of mind. It did not take long, however, for the quality of Dyfan's writing and the emotional kick of this exquisite human drama to come under my guard, disarm me and leave me feeling child-like and exposed. Even though I blubbed my way through much of the book, I found myself strangely nourished, humbled and uplifted by the experience. In my reply to Dyfan's request for feedback, I wrote:

> I loved what the memoir did to me as a human, a father, a husband and as a follower of Jesus. It is wholesome but not comfortable, brutally honest and yet orthodox;... the brutal reality of bereavement and a sense of my own mortality cast me onto my heavenly Father...'

The structure of the book is simple and profound. For the most part, it tells the story sequentially and allows the reader to eve's drop on the main protagonist's thoughts and feelings. Both the real-time and subsequent reflections that intersperse the events, add depth and colour to what would otherwise be a simple and tragic story.

Shock, Tears, Groaning, Hope, Darkness, Anger, Longing, Why?, Futility, Heaven and Glory along with the other section headings provide clear signposting and pace to the book. The inclusion of poetry, including some of the author's own compositions, is beautifully and instructively done; forcing the reader to pause and reflect deeply rather than simply be told what to think.

The author states his aim in the preface:

> My prayer is that God will use this book to help others —both those who may be called to walk through

similar dark valleys and those who are called to offer comfort by walking with them.

Dyfan has certainly provided the church with a resource that offers comfort to those devastated by bereavement and also helps Christians to be a source of comfort rather than discouragement, by avoiding those well-meant spiritual sayings that can unintentionally minimise the grief of the bereaved. The main value of the book however, is found not so much in the utility of the didactic passages, insightful and helpful as they are, but rather in the beautifully crafted, brutally honest reflections on the grief of losing a beloved child.

To truly flourish in our lives and relationships, inside and outside the church, we must properly embrace our humanity rather than adopt an 'acceptable' posture that we wish to project outwardly. In the following pages we are provided with a model of what that can look like. It is not easy, comfortable or neat, but it is biblical, humanising and ultimately glorifying to God.

Richard Cunningham, Director of UCCF

ACKNOWLEDGMENTS

The writing of this book demanded a great amount of energy and would never have been accomplished without the encouragement, tenacity and support of so many people. I want to acknowledge some of them here.

Caroline, you deserve first mention, for being so persistently positive about this venture, stretching over many years. Thank you for your love and for keeping me going when I would have given up.

Elspeth, you were the first to read the original manuscript. Your sympathetic response and insightful comments in those very early stages gave me the courage to continue.

Wes and Karen, for your faithful friendship and strong support over many years, from the days when we were ten and long before.

Trevor and Jo, our dear friends and fellow mourners, thank you for your love and enthusiasm.

Bruce and Linda, thank you for your warm and generous Connecticut hospitality, providing a beautiful setting for the final stages of writing.

Auntie Brenda, for your brilliant editorial skills, sharp-sightedness, willing work and loving prayers.

The leaders and members of Emmanuel Church, Leftwich, for giving me a sabbatical, without which the book would never have been completed.

Elinor, Eryl, Phil, Ray, Richard and Sinclair, for taking time to read my words and write such kind ones in return.

PREFACE

To begin at the beginning...

The train now standing at platform 2 is the 17:15 to
Shrewsbury, calling at Wrexham, Ruabon, Chirk,
Gobowen and Shrewsbury; connections at
Shrewsbury for Wolverhampton, Birmingham New
Street, and Birmingham International.

As a teenager, I had memorised this public
announcement, having heard it so many times while
waiting to catch the train from Chester to Ruabon, the
village where I grew up. Ruabon lies about five miles
south of Wrexham, nestled in the top right-hand corner
of Wales. It has two primary schools: the County Primary
and St Mary's Church of England. I attended the former,

along with my three brothers. We did not care much for those at St Mary's. They were the 'posh' kids, we believed; and we were not 'posh'! There was, however, only one secondary school, Ysgol Rhiwabon, where the posh and not-so-posh pupils would meet and mingle. It was here that I played football for the school team, the trumpet in the school band, and developed an interest in English literature. This was mainly due to a new teacher in my fourth year who had the daunting task of introducing the class to Shakespeare's *Julius Caesar* and some twentieth-century poetry. My mum, who always cherished a love for literature, encouraged in me an appreciation for the written word. So perhaps there was no great surprise when eventually I ventured south to study English literature at the University of Wales, Cardiff.

In the August of 1989, before entering my final year as a student, I met Caroline at Aberystwyth. We were introduced through some mutual friends who were all attending the long-standing Christian conference organised by the Evangelical Movement of Wales. Caroline had just qualified as an Occupational Therapist and had moved down from her home in Glasgow to live and work in Chorley, Lancashire. It was not quite love at first sight on my part, as she sometimes reminds me, but by the end of the week I was smitten! In the September she drove over to Ruabon to celebrate my twenty-first birthday. We watched *Othello* at Theatre Clwyd and as that did not seem to put her off, our relationship developed through frequent letters, long phone calls (land-line, of course) and occasional weekend visits. A year later, at the same Aberystwyth conference, we were engaged. We married in Glasgow in May, 1991.

We settled in the lovely county of Lancashire. We enjoyed the people's distinctive accent, along with their warmth and humour. My first job was at the Chorley Employment Service Job Centre as an Administrative Assistant. Nearly two years later I sensed a call from God towards Christian ministry and applied to be a Staff Worker for UCCF. This involved travelling to various universities and colleges in Lancashire, encouraging and training students as they organised and led their Christian Unions. The Lord opened the door leading to three stimulating years in the student world. Following this, God opened another door, leading me to serve as co-pastor of Grace Baptist Church, Southport. I was to work alongside an experienced pastor, Peter Day. Through his wisdom and experience I would learn so much about the pastoral ministry. During the autumn of 1995 we made the move from Chorley to Southport, towns separated by about twenty miles, but so unlike in many ways. Southport seemed to be more affluent; a flat, sea-side town, where people came to retire. It would be our home for the next eleven years. By now, God had blessed us with two young children: Megan, aged two-and-a-half, and Lloyd, just six months.

The Lord was also blessing the church, and the congregation continued to grow. We had been called to serve young families and young people, and it was wonderfully exciting to see the way the Lord began to work among these age groups. Our days were very busy and hectic as we juggled the demands of church ministry with the energy required in raising a young family. In 1998 God blessed us with our third child, Sian, born in Southport hospital. So in the space of five years we had become a family of five. Caroline and I regard all three children as God's gifts, equally precious to us and to him. Yet something would happen in 2003 that would affect our family and faith profoundly. This book is a personal account of what happened that year, my own experience and reflections upon some of the many facets of grief and faith, loss and hope.

My hope and prayer is that God will use this book to bring help to those who may be called to walk through similar dark valleys; to those who are called to offer comfort by walking with them; and to those who would like to know more about the hope that can be found through Jesus Christ.

Blessed be the God and Father of our Lord Jesus Christ, the Father of mercies and God of all comfort, who comforts us in all our affliction, so that we may be able to comfort those who are in any affliction.

— 2 CORINTHIANS 1:3-4

1

BEGINNINGS

My heart leaps up when I behold
A rainbow in the sky:
So was it when my life began;
So is it now I am a man;
So be it when I shall grow old,
Or let me die!

— WILLIAM WORDSWORTH

I sat in the corner, like a silent spectator, and stared at the screen, but inside I was praying and willing the figures upwards into the 'safety zone', as the nurse had described it. White-coated medics, wearing anxious expressions, flocked around the bed. My fears, like a see-saw, rose and fell with those numbers. The heart-beat was weakening. I thought of those who would be praying for us: my parents, Caroline's parents, our brothers, sisters and friends. Was this scene real, or just some terrible nightmare? How would it end? I fought to suppress that terrifying train of thought and re-focused on the monitor. Finally, with a heroic effort from Caroline, along with the doctor's assistance, our first baby was born! The long, protracted labour, with all its pain and fear, gave way to relief and rejoicing!

In this way Megan Ruth Williams entered this world and our lives, at precisely 1.53am on March 8th 1993. I remember holding her for the first time, her tiny face protruding from the standard issue orange hospital blanket, her eyes barely open. I remember hearing her first cry—not angry or fretful, but gentle, delicate, like the bleating of a new-born lamb. Wonder and excitement enveloped me as I gazed down at this precious, tiny form. Was she really mine? Could it be true? We were the proud parents of a beautiful daughter. I was a father!

Driving home through empty streets at about 4am, with little regard for speed limits, I was possessed by joy. Spontaneous praise to the Lord welled up within me for his goodness and mercy: Caroline and Megan were safe and well. It was a miracle. *Megan*: the sound of her name was just beginning to flow naturally from my lips. How different the outcome might have been! On many subsequent occasions, suddenly aware of our great privilege to be parents, I would ask myself, "Why should the Lord have given her to us?" She was not ours by right, but a gift from God. After a few hours' sleep the day began with phone calls to so many glad and grateful recipients of our good news. I recall pushing Megan in the buggy for the first time. In the local park there was an avenue of cherry trees and in the brilliant sunlight of that March day it was as though their vibrant, pink blossom, like a candyfloss celebration, was displayed just for us. Somehow, everywhere nature's colours shone significantly brighter. These were blessed and happy days, days when I began to view the world through Megan's eyes and felt what William Wordsworth had tried to capture in his poetry, the extraordinary in the ordinary.

Sunflowers

During those years as a young family, we usually holidayed in Wales. Pembrokeshire was a favourite destination, with its beautiful beaches and gorgeous greenery. We always went with our good friends, Wes and Karen, mutual friends who had brought us together. They had married a couple of years before us, and had also settled in Chorley. It was not planned but our children came along consecutively and we became very close as families, spending some memorable holidays together in Wales. But after a few years we realised that Pembrokeshire in August was not always as warm and sunny as we hoped, and we were spending extra money on rainy days trying to entertain six lively children! So one summer we decided to venture into France. We held out the hope that the sun would always be shining in Brittany! It was quite an adventure as we drove through the night to Weymouth to catch the ferry across to St Malo. Despite the white-knuckle ride for the first few minutes after leaving the ferry—we had never driven on the 'wrong' side of the road before!—we soon settled down and began to enjoy the experience of our first holiday abroad.

The next year we gained more confidence and ventured slightly further south, towards La Rochelle. It was here that we first witnessed the glorious spectacle of fields upon fields of sunflowers, with their heads tilting in unison towards the sun. I discovered later that sunflowers, as they grow, tilt during the day to face the sun, but stop once they begin blooming. Mature sunflowers generally face east, as though looking expectantly each day for the sunrise. I think we all fell in love with the sight, and the sunflower immediately became Megan's favourite flower. Megan loved beauty and art, music and drama, stories and books. She was a sociable child and in some ways through her sunny and sensitive disposition, for me she resembled the sunflower. Blake's poem, *Ah! Sun-flower*, expresses the mixture of beauty, longing and hope that the sight of a sunflower still evokes in me today as it seems to count "the steps of the Sun", searching for that happy destination—that "sweet golden clime"—"Where the traveller's journey is done".

2

EMERGENCY

He holds him with his glitt'ring
    eye–
The Wedding-Guest stood still,
And listens like a three years' child:
The Mariner hath his will.
The Wedding-Guest sat on a stone:
He cannot choose but hear;
And thus spake on that ancient
    man,
The bright-eyed Mariner.

— WILLIAM COLERIDGE

Back in school we studied Coleridge's famous poem, *The*

Rhyme of the Ancient Mariner. Here at the beginning we find the mariner stopping a complete stranger, a wedding guest, to tell him the dramatic tale of his experiences at sea. I feel a little like the mariner, though hopefully not quite as ancient, as I attempt to begin my story.

It was a Monday, March 24th 2003 in Southport. Megan returned home from school complaining of a sore head, vague about the details but said that it had happened during a PE lesson towards the end of the school day. My parents had travelled over from North Wales to visit and had collected our three children from school. It had been Lloyd's eighth birthday the day before, and Mum and Dad were planning to take both Megan and Lloyd to the shops to get them each a present. Siân, our youngest, had just turned five in February. That day was important for another reason. Megan was going to sit her grade 1 piano exam just after 5pm. She had been preparing for this for several months, and that day—the day she had somewhat dreaded—had now arrived. I had been trying to help her with her sight-reading during the previous week. She had improved a little, and her piano teacher was due to call at the house for a final practice at 4pm. It was going to be a busy few hours.

I remember greeting Megan with my usual hug in the hall, just outside my study. "Dad, my head's sore," she said, almost immediately. I said something about 'giving it a rub and it'll get better'—my usual response to minor aches and scrapes. Caroline confirmed that Megan had hurt her head; she had received a note from the school to say so. But thoughts of the piano exam came to the fore and we sent Megan upstairs to change out of her school uniform while Dad and I went out with Lloyd to a side street. We wanted to see him try out his birthday present, a new skateboard. Lloyd was a little uncertain on the board, and kept falling off. Finally, with all the frustration an eight-year-old could muster, he threw the skateboard away and stormed off into the house. Dad and I returned too. By this time Megan's piano teacher had arrived to help her prepare for the exam. She cried during the practice and the teacher expressed concern that Megan was complaining of a pain in her head. Lloyd descended from his bedroom somewhat embarrassed by his recent failure and loss of temper. I tried a joke in an attempt to snap him out of his mood, but unsuccessfully! Suddenly, Caroline called me from the kitchen. Her tone alarmed me, and I could see Megan leaning limply against her.

Hospital

Caroline judged that we had better get Megan to casualty, so we made some hasty arrangements and drove to the hospital. Caroline was sitting in the back of the car with Megan. I can recall the conversation: I could hear Caroline's questions, but it was clear that Megan could not. "What did you say?" she kept asking. She was becoming incoherent as she drifted in and out of consciousness. I now realised that this had nothing to do with pre-piano exam nerves. Leaving Caroline and Megan at the Accident and Emergency entrance I went to park the car. Then I hurried to the waiting room, but was unable to find them. "Are you looking for anyone, love?" a member of staff inquired. "Yes! My wife and daughter!" "They're through in that first room on the right." Later, I learned that when Caroline had mentioned 'head injury' the nurse had ushered them through immediately. The little room in which I found them was obviously for children. Disney cartoon characters decorated the walls. Megan had been delighted by many of them, but now she was lying still, with Caroline by her side.

It seems strange now, but at this point I was not too anxious. I expected that Megan was, at worst, a little concussed; that they would observe her, and then send her home with instructions to 'keep an eye on her.' Perhaps they would require her to stay in hospital overnight, and therefore probably Caroline would remain with her. My thoughts turned to the church members' meeting arranged for that evening which I was supposed to be leading. I decided to call my colleague to prepare him for taking over this responsibility. On returning to the little ward, efforts were being made to talk to Megan. It was as though she was far away and could barely hear our voices. The nurse did not seem too perturbed that Megan was drifting off to sleep. "We'll just keep waking her to take her blood pressure," she said. An Indian lady doctor entered, her accent was not easy to understand. "What exactly happened?" We repeated the details—the series of events that had led up to this point, including approximate times. She addressed Megan with a pronounced Indian accent: "What is your name?" "Megan." "And your surname?" Megan did not seem to understand, probably due to the accent, I guessed. "Megan what?" I interjected, trying to clarify. "Williams," came her reply. "And what did you have for lunch today?" At this, Megan gave us one of her quizzical looks, as if to say, "What kind of a silly question is that?!" It was so funny, both Caroline and I laughed spontaneously. "Do you know where you are?" The questions kept coming. "Here!" Megan replied. "Where is 'here'?" "Here...in this dead place." We have often wondered where that answer came from. What did she mean by such an unusual phrase? Did she have a perception of what was coming? "And where is your daddy?" the doctor persisted. At this Megan scanned the room. She saw me and pointed, "There!" So it was in a hospital, across a small children's room, while drifting in and out of consciousness, Megan identified me as her father. I will never forget it.

3

SHOCK

Megan began to panic, suddenly feeling that she needed the toilet. A bed pan was called for as she fumbled with her clothing, her favourite purple velvet trousers. But it was a false alarm. On a couple of occasions she called out in fear, wanting her mum. Caroline was always near at hand to comfort and reassure her. It was decided to move us into another room, less child-friendly, more clinical. Again, Megan became agitated about relieving herself. Again it was a false alarm. We decided to undress her, just in case. In an effort to relieve some tension I joked to Megan about her smelly socks. Immediately I sensed from the nurse that jokes were no longer appropriate. The situation was becoming serious and I regretted my flippancy.

An X-ray was suggested, to see if there was any sign of a fracture. We both followed Megan as she was pushed on a trolley along the hospital corridor, but only Caroline was allowed into the room. I stood outside, praying intensely. There was nothing else to do; they would be the first of many prayers. Afterwards it was back to another bay, with curtains for walls, and more doctors. Now we were very worried, clinging to each other as we witnessed our precious daughter lying motionless, unresponsive. At this point I felt like breaking down in tears. I held Caroline tightly and whispered in her ear, "The Lord's in control. We must trust him." We prayed. More doctors appeared, one young and tall, another older, in a grey suit, foreign, another darker, Indian perhaps. The urgency was palpable. We were horrified spectators, shocked like rabbits caught in the headlights, fearful now that something terrible was looming towards us. I saw the grey-suited doctor pressing his thumb deep into Megan's forehead, hoping she would react. He turned to apologise to us, as though suddenly realising how disturbing the sight must have been, but Megan had made no response.

I phoned a friend from church for the school teachers' numbers. "Just pray!" I managed to say, choking back my tears. I called the teachers, trying to learn more about what exactly had happened to Megan at school. No-one seemed to know for sure. The teacher said Megan had complained that she had been hit on the back of her head, but the staff members were certain that had not happened. Megan was taken into another room, more like an intensive care unit. There I believe she was placed on a ventilator: Caroline and I waited outside, not wanting to witness this. The small Indian doctor came out to us and spoke calmly and carefully, explaining what was happing to our daughter. We just listened, paralysed by shock and unable to form any questions of our own.

We were now in the hands of others. A nurse led us down another corridor and showed us into a small room with just enough space for a sofa, a cabinet and telephone. Here we waited, clinging to each other. I recognised this place; I had been here before, just a few months earlier, trying to console the bereaved relatives of a man who had died very suddenly. Now *we* were here! It was as though a film were being shown before our eyes, but with the horrifying sense that we were playing the parts. Left alone we stared at each other, attempting to absorb what we had just experienced. Despite our fears we talked quietly and prayed together. The Lord was our only source of help.

Finally, a group of hospital staff crammed into the small room with us: the grey-suited man, the nurse, the small Indian doctor. Megan had undergone a brain scan, the grey-suited man explained, and the results revealed a bleed in the left side. The decision had been made to send her to the Walton Centre in Liverpool. An ambulance was ordered, along with a police escort. As I replay this scene I feel I ought to have been crying out in anguish, "How could this be happening?!" But nothing was said—the shock had numbed us into silence.

Ambulance

We were not allowed to accompany Megan in the ambulance, but the kind Indian doctor seemed sensitive to our feelings and, along with the nurse, clarified the details we needed to know. We left that little room and returned to find Megan. What a sight greeted us! She was linked to a ventilator, with several other tubes attaching her to various pieces of equipment. It was a horrendous scene. The Indian doctor spoke calmly to us as we waited for Megan to be transferred. The sight of her as she was wheeled past and through the emergency doors was almost too much for us to bear. "Just trust the Lord" were the Indian doctor's parting words. "We will," replied Caroline. I could say nothing. Caroline recalls an African doctor, dressed in a white coat—the rest were in scrubs —whom we had never seen before. He held the door open as Megan was pushed through, looked directly at Caroline, saying, "The Lord is with you," and Caroline replied, "I know he is." She believes this person could well have been an angel sent especially to give words of comfort and strength at just the right time.

En route to Liverpool I had the presence of mind to remember that the Walton Centre was now in its new setting next to Fazakerley Hospital. Thankfully I knew where to go since I had visited someone there not so long before, and during the summer holidays we had met my parents in that very hospital car park and collected the three children following a stay with them in North Wales. How different things were now! On our arrival we learned that Megan had already been rushed into the hospital. The two of us made our way into the lounge for relatives. We sat and waited. Caroline's sister, and a friend, were already there, their faces pale and drawn. The silent waiting began.

> Hear my cry, O God,
> listen to my prayer;
> from the end of the earth I call
>   to you
> when my heart is faint.
> Lead me to the rock
> that is higher than I,
> for you have been my refuge,
> a strong tower against the enemy
>
> — PSALM 61:1-3

4

OPERATION

There was little to say. A nurse entered and spoke quietly with us. She needed to know some details and facts about Megan: full name, date and place of birth; information that became even more precious to us now. The nurse left and in came a surgeon, gowned for theatre. He was foreign, East-European I guessed from his accent. He explained that a second scan had revealed a large bleed in the left-hand side of Megan's brain caused by a sub-arachnoid haemorrhage. He needed to operate to remove the clot, but it was a life-threatening procedure. Would I sign a consent form? I did so without hesitation. What else could I do? My mind went back to the night of Megan's birth. She was no more than an hour old when I was asked to give medical consent for a particular treatment. I remember realising then that fatherhood brought major responsibility: decision-making for someone else's life! But I had never expected this. Did we have any questions? I asked about the length of the operation, but that was all. Perhaps I should have mentioned our faith in the Lord, for that was certainly what I was relying on: "This man is a skilled surgeon, but the Lord—the Great Physician—can guide and help him." But such thoughts melted away before becoming words.

We waited, heads bowed in silent prayer, while time passed slowly. Another nurse arrived to supply more information and confirm more details. She left, leaving us to absorb the nightmare of the last six or eight hours; our disbelief and anxiety had heightened with each successive stage of Megan's decline. Another man came to speak with us—we would learn later that he was the anaesthetist, Mr. T. He was dressed in blue operating theatre 'scrubs' with a pink hat. He spoke quietly, succinctly, measuring each word as he reported that the operation had taken place. It was too soon to tell how successful it had been, his manner revealing the uncertainty of Megan's future. She would now be moved to intensive care. For a while Caroline and I were alone in the family room, but then two ladies entered looking tired and anxious. They spoke quietly to one another, but I detected a Welsh accent and took the courage to open up a conversation. They were from Tenby, South

Wales. The older woman was the mother of a young man who had just undergone an eight-hour operation to remove a tumour from his brain. The younger lady was his wife, married to him for just a couple of years. The mother seemed strong emotionally and spoke with us as we managed to share something of our story. It was as though the Lord had provided her reassuring presence to help us at this time. In her exhaustion the young wife just sank into a chair and slept.

The surgeon came to see us and explained how he had removed a blood clot from the left side of Megan's brain. We had no questions, but thanked him sincerely for his efforts. At some point we had been informed that the left side of the brain was responsible for much of the correct functioning of the body. Perhaps we were being prepared for the likelihood that, if Megan were to survive, she would have severe problems. We were too numb to assimilate this information and process its consequences at the time. A nurse arrived and began to prepare us to see Megan by explaining that there would be lots of tubes and machines. We listened with increasing anxiety to see her, mixed with the fear of what that sight would bring. Finally we were allowed to enter the ward.

There she lay, amidst a mass of machines, tubes, wires, monitors and a ventilator. Part of her head had been shaved and there were traces of blood. But her face, her freckles, her tanned skin (a little reminder of our last holiday in Florida), arms and legs remained the same, so beautifully precious and familiar. She lay as she had slept at home: straight-backed, facing the ceiling, eyes closed. How we longed to embrace her! We wept. Caroline spoke to Megan through her tears and sobs; I could only manage to whisper in her ear. This was all too much to take in. For the next ten days the noise of the ventilator and occasional bleeps of a monitor would become familiar sounds.

Tears

Although there were three or four other bays in the ward, no-one else would be treated there for the length of Megan's stay. The place became like a private room and we were grateful, but, for that night only, a young child was brought in to occupy a bed. She was crying and very distressed, and by the grating sound at each intake of breath I thought she must have had a tracheotomy. The cries of this little one distressed me, but the nurses remained calm while the helpless mother looked on. I consoled myself with the thought that Megan was not experiencing this kind of trauma—at least she appeared peaceful.

It must have been well past midnight when we finally lay down to sleep in a side ward, near to Megan. In our exhaustion we committed her and ourselves to the Lord and tried to sleep. Caroline was unable to settle for a long time and when I awoke after four or five hours, I found her in a chair next to Megan's bed, her head resting near Megan's side, where she had been for most of the night. Megan had made it through to the morning, Tuesday 25th March.

We endured the next ten days in that hospital with the help of one another, the medical staff, our family and friends, the prayers of God's people in Southport and all over the world, and the Lord himself, whose grace carried us through. I think the staff would not have been surprised if Megan died during that first night in hospital, but she was, in a sense, still with us. So a plan was put into action, beginning with another brain scan to discover how successful the operation had been. By now, news had travelled and people were beginning to pray. My parents joined us at the hospital once Lloyd and Siân had gone to school. Our close friends, Wes and Karen, came from Chorley. They were to be a tower of strength for us in the days ahead. Caroline's parents, now living in America, had been contacted. Her father managed to call the ward from Florida. I remember how his voice trembled on the phone and I too could hardly speak. They were going to take a flight as soon as possible and planned to arrive on Wednesday morning. Wesley asked the staff for a private room where we could all meet, and we were shown into an empty side ward where the kind staff served us with tea and coffee. We waited for the result from the scan.

Finally, Caroline and I were shown into a small nurse's office. There, Mr. B, the paediatrician, along with the head nurse spoke to us. It was a tight squeeze for four people. Caroline and I took our seats. Mr. B was a relatively young man, built like a second row rugby forward. He began by explaining to us all that had happened to Megan, underlining the seriousness of her condition. I remember Caroline rocking slightly back and forth, her eyes fixed on a point on the floor, while she braced herself for this latest news. I attempted to maintain eye-contact while Mr. B explained how the scan had revealed that Megan had suffered a sub-arachnoid haemorrhage, which was nothing to do with a bump on the head, yet that may have been how it felt to her when it occurred. The pressure of the bleed had caused a severe amount of damage. From contrasting x-ray pictures he showed us what ought to be there, and what was missing for Megan. He was painting a bleak picture. The brain stem may have been damaged irreparably, which meant certain death. He explained that it could have happened at any time, when she was six or sixty. "If Megan were to survive," he explained, "the likelihood would be that her life would be very limited. She'll never go to school and never get a job..." Until then Mr. B had been striving to speak objectively, but at this point he paused and I noticed tears welling up in his eyes. I will never forget him for this: his tears were an eloquent testimony to his sympathy for us as we received his devastating news. He wiped them away and continued. The plan would be to monitor Megan in the hope that the ominous signs of increasing pressure in her brain (indicated by the swelling of her pupils) would diminish. If so, then a probe would be inserted into her brain to measure the pressure more accurately. There was no hope of performing a second operation; the internal pressure was too great.

> I am weary with my moaning;
> every night I flood my bed with
>   tears;
> I drench my couch with my
>   weeping.
> My eye wastes away because of
>   grief;
> it grows weak because of all my
>   foes.

> — PSALM 6:6-7

Some of us shed tears more readily than others. Some still hear the words of disapproval: "Big boys don't cry!" David was not ashamed to admit to crying, and he was by no means a weakling! If you are walking a painful path at this moment, shedding tears may be just the right thing to do. David was not ashamed of his tears. He also realised that the LORD was not ashamed of them either, but remembered them with tenderness and sympathy:

> You have... put my tears in your
>   bottle.
> Are they not in your book?
>
> — PSALM 56:8

5

GROANING

We had hoped for something more positive, but now we knew the truth and instinctively we felt that we were being prepared for the worst. Questions formed quickly in my mind: had Megan already died en route to Liverpool, perhaps even in Southport? Was it clutching at straws to hold out hope of her recovery? Mr. B had mentioned doing tests to detect any signs of life, once the medication was withdrawn, and at this moment we faced and felt the reality of death. Having been left alone, we clung to each other in the hospital corridor and wept, assuring one another in whispered sobs that the Lord had taken her to a better place, away from this sad and sinful world. We had enjoyed ten happy years with her, and she with us. At the approach of this storm the Lord was sustaining us with his grace. We would stand in need of much more grace in the days to come.

A nurse guided us to a private room while Mr. B went to inform our family and friends. There he described the surgeon's efforts as 'heroic' because he personally would not have attempted the surgery had he been on call that evening; and confessed that Megan was in 'higher hands.' What was to be done? How does one continue to function when such devastating news has just been received? Somehow a plan was put in place. Friends arranged to collect Lloyd and Siân from school, take them for tea, and gently try to impress upon them the seriousness of Megan's condition. A little later I left for home with my parents to collect some clothes and see Lloyd and Siân. We did not speak much on the journey. My thoughts and feelings were convincing me that Megan had died. I stared out at the hedgerows and fields beyond. What would life be without her? How would we survive her loss? Was all this real? As real as the sun shining down so brightly upon us that afternoon, and the spring flowers just beginning to bloom?

We arrived at our empty home and I took a shower. As the warm water flowed over me my numbed emotions began to melt. Then a deep, deep groaning came from within me. It was a feeling I had never experienced before. The enormity of her loss was only just beginning to dawn upon me and I moaned out my grief. This was the bathroom in which I had bathed Megan so many times. This was the place where I had knelt and we had talked together. She would cover her eyes while I rinsed her hair. There on the wall hung her colourful fish picture. I wandered into other rooms. Inevitably, so many objects evoked memories of Megan. Is this how it was going to be? Just memories and pain? Megan may have been taken to heaven but I wanted her here with me!

The children arrived and greeted me with warm hugs and kisses. It was so good to touch, hold and hear them. Their pleasure in seeing me was some comfort. I decided to speak with them alone in our bedroom. How do you explain such things to an eight and five-year-old? I told them that Megan was now in the hospital in Liverpool and that she was very ill. "Is she going to die?" asked Lloyd, clearly understanding more than Siân. "We don't know what the Lord Jesus will do yet. He may take her to be with him or make her better so she can stay with us." I had not given up hope completely. They asked me questions about heaven, and Lloyd particularly became upset and began to cry.

Care

On returning to the hospital that evening I learned that a family room had been made available for us, just across the corridor from the intensive care unit: two single beds, a wardrobe, chair and sink. We were grateful for this provision.

Wednesday morning saw the arrival of Caroline's parents from Florida; their faces were grey with anguish.

We all burst into tears as we greeted them at the door of the ward. Before they went to see Megan, we met in a small side room to explain Megan's condition. Caroline remained calm as she narrated the details but mum and dad were engulfed with grief. Eventually they went in to see their beloved grand-daughter. The sight for them, I think, was almost too much to bear. She lay, amidst machinery and medicine, motionless apart from the rhythmic rising and falling of her chest as the ventilator did its work.

That day brought about a slight but significant change in us. Though we were never far removed from the realisation that Megan's state was critical, we were prepared to take encouragement from any slight improvements: from blood pressure, oxygen levels, or any of the other readings we were beginning to learn from the monitor above Megan's bed. This was the beginning of our emotional roller-coaster ride, with the highs of hope and lows of fear, and with no option to disembark. That night a fire alarm woke everyone at 2am. Fire fighters arrived as we hurried across to the ward, but there was no fire. It was a false alarm; an emergency we did not need. We made our way back to the room and drifted off to sleep.

Thursday morning saw cards and letters begin to pour in for Megan and for us. Our news was spreading and so many people were praying for us! Despite the traumatic state we were in, we were managing to sleep well. Nevertheless, each morning would dawn with the reality of Megan's critical condition and we would return to our place at her side. Had there been any change for the better during the night? Not really. Our hearts would sink again under the weight of worry. Megan's medication was keeping her heavily sedated to allow her brain the maximum opportunity to rest and recover. Today she would be sent for another brain scan, since she had been unstable during the night. The doctors needed to know if there had been another bleed. I could not bear the thought of more pressure building up inside her head; it pained me to dwell upon it, and I could not watch as three or four nurses transferred Megan carefully onto a trolley to take her for the scan. All I could do was entrust her to the Lord and to the skill of the medical team.

Hope

As time slowly passed we began to build relationships with the staff, especially the nurses, who cared for Megan with great diligence and dignity. The scan, we were told, had revealed no change. I returned to Southport that evening with a heavy heart. *How long, O Lord?* Both sets of parents were present for the evening meal when a phone call came through from the hospital. It was Caroline with news from Mr. B, the paediatrician. He had just examined the scan for himself and announced that we had been misinformed; there *were* signs of some improvement! We trembled as we spoke with him! Then I broke the good news to our parents and could hardly contain my emotions. We all shed tears of relief and hope. Mr. B's prediction of a "long campaign" at the beginning of the week was proving to be right, but now we had a glimmer of hope and we were clinging to it tenaciously. What else was there to do?

Church members and friends had begun to gather each evening at the church to pray for Megan. We were told later how these had been exceptional meetings. Several non-Christian friends, some who would not normally have been found in a church, including teachers from her school, made the effort to join with the faithful folks at 'Grace.' The news of hope from the scan would have been conveyed to the meeting that evening. We can only imagine what the reaction must have been and how our friends were spurred on to pray. In addition to this prayer support it was comforting to have our family around us.

On the Friday morning Megan seemed to be more stable. She was connected to another machine to monitor her brain activity. Now there was another set of figures to watch! Frequent measurements were made of Megan's blood gases; her pupils were checked regularly for size and movement. I believe they were always unresponsive, though after each check I studied the nurse's face for any signs of hope. Sometimes Megan's oxygen levels would dip and she would require physiotherapy to clear her lungs. A physiotherapist would arrive to do the delicate task and at this point we would leave. Although we knew it was necessary, it was simply too distressing to witness our own daughter's fragile frame being worked upon in this way. Visitors came and went. The ward's 'teenager room' became our unofficial base, since nobody else was using it. There was a TV, video player and some soft chairs. We would also venture into the 'courtyard' area to breathe some fresh air or buy refreshments from the adjoining café. A fountain flowed in the centre of the courtyard garden and that became a symbol of hope. I believed that God was the fountain of all life, and that he could keep Megan alive, if he willed. How I longed that he would!

> Why is light given to a man
>   whose way is hidden,
> whom God has hedged in?
> For my sighing comes instead of
>   my bread,
> and my groanings are poured out
>   like water.
> For the thing that I fear comes
>   upon me,
> and what I dread befalls me.
> I am not at ease, nor am I quiet;
> I have no rest, but trouble comes.

— JOB 3:23-26

The book of Job has been a source of help to so many who experience suffering of various kinds. If you can identify with the description of his "groanings" and "dread", and if you are "not at ease" and "have no rest", then reading through the book of Job may be just what you need.

6

MIRACLE

Despite our hopes and prayers, Megan became alarmingly unstable on Saturday morning. My parents visited that day and I stood with Dad in the corridor, looking onto the courtyard garden. He mentioned the passage in the Gospels where the Roman centurion had approached Jesus out of great concern for his sick servant. Jesus was on his way to the house, but then the centurion said to him, "Just say the word and my servant will be healed." Jesus was astonished by such great faith from a Gentile. Surely the Lord could just "say the word" and heal Megan. Surely this is what we were asking him to do and we also believed that he could do it.

Megan's oxygen levels were decreasing rapidly. The anaesthetist on duty grew more and more concerned. Various attempts were made to stabilise her, but with no response. The anaesthetist called his colleague at Alder

Hey Hospital to ask about alternative options and eventually a proposal was made: Megan could be transferred from the Walton Centre to Alder Hey hospital where she could be placed on a different type of ventilator. It might just work, though there were definite risks involved in moving her. The decision was ours: what should we do? We had precious little option, so I agreed.

It was evening and people were beginning to gather at the church for their regular time of prayer for us and someone informed them of the crisis we were in. Caroline and I rushed back to our room and began frantically to pack our belongings in preparation for the move. Was this the time we had dreaded? Would all this effort be in vain? Fear and faith like two torrents clashed and flowed within me. At this point Wesley came from the ward with some astonishing news. As the staff had transferred Megan onto the portable ventilator in preparation for the journey, her figures had improved dramatically! Soon, the anaesthetist came looking for us. Sitting down upon the bed, bemused and relieved, he tried to explain the sequence of events. "I do not know why or how this has happened, but Megan has suddenly become more balanced." The immediate crisis was over, there was no reason now why we should move to Alder Hey. Megan would remain on the portable ventilator for the time being. Caroline and I looked at each other: we were convinced that this had been the work of God in answer to prayer. We sent news back to the church prayer meeting, and again, we can only imagine the thanksgiving and praise that was offered up to the Lord that night! We were thankful too. The Lord had brought us to the very brink, but drew us back again. We spoke about the power of prayer to the staff. I really do not know what they thought of us, but we cared little about that. Now we had reason to hope.

Mother's Day

Sunday was Mother's Day. How could we face it? The Lord had given us the ability to sleep reasonably well each night. We slept with the knowledge that loving friends or family members would be sitting with Megan through the darkness. But how would we face today? Megan seemed fairly stable, at least compared to yesterday, so we decided that Caroline and I would return home for lunch and the afternoon. A friend from church agreed willingly to remain with Megan. Her husband brought her to the hospital and then took us back in his car. The sight of the beautiful, sunny day brought us a measure of relief from the intense atmosphere of the ward. We gazed upon green fields and colourful flowers and saw daffodils blooming on roadside verges. All around us nature was springing to life, but the heaviness lodged in our hearts remained.

Mother's Day it was, yet our daughter's life hung in the balance.

The family greeted us at home: Lloyd and Siân, our parents and other family members. They were all determined to keep our spirits up, as were we, for the sake of the children. Siân had bought a toy, a musical Ostrich, at an event in her school. The tune and humorous dance of the bird provided a welcome distraction as the children laughed, but someone precious was missing. It had been a marvellous Mother's Day dinner, and afterwards we spent time in the garden, playing games with the kids in the sunshine. Was this right? Should we be playing while Megan lay in hospital? Caroline found the day particularly painful. Everyone did their best to remain positive, but it was difficult. We were grateful for such a loving, supportive family, united in anxiety, sustained by faith. In the evening, back at the hospital, a little boy had made Caroline a Mother's Day card, and gave it to her, since, he said, he knew Megan could not make her one.

Prayer Square

The next day Megan's figures remained stable. By now we were becoming adept at reading the various monitors. We knew what was good and bad, but I could only sit and watch them for so long. When certain figures rose into the danger-zone, an alarm would sound to notify the nurse. My own heart would race with fear.

I took myself out through the rear entrance of the hospital. There, near the car park, I found a square of grass bordered by a path of concrete slabs. This place became my personal 'prayer square.' I was convicted. I knew that so many people around the world were praying fervently for Megan, yet up to now I had not set aside time to do the same. Of course, I had been praying, but quickly and often, usually at Megan's bedside or in our room. The intensity of our situation had made it difficult to concentrate on anything, even prayer. But now, like Jacob in Genesis, I resolved to wrestle with God. I would plead his promises. The problem was that, deep down in my heart, I knew that God had not promised to heal my daughter. I was aware of general promises in God's Word to his believing people, but none could assure me specifically that Megan would recover. However, I reminded myself that there were many instances in the Gospels where Jesus commended people for their faith. The Roman centurion had astonished Jesus with his confidence: *...only say the word, and my servant will be healed* (Matthew 8:8). The sick woman who had pushed her way through the crowd to touch the hem of Jesus' garment, believing that she would be healed by his power, was commended by the Lord: *Daughter, your faith has made you well; go in peace, and be healed of your disease.* (Mark 5:34). More significantly, Jairus, the synagogue ruler, had pleaded earnestly with Jesus to come and heal his twelve year-old daughter: *Come and lay your hands on her, so that she may be made well and live* (Mark 5:23). Jesus had responded to his cry and I clung to these examples.

I had often been inspired by the faith of Shadrach, Meshach and Abednego in the book of Daniel. They were threatened with death in the blazing furnace by King Nebuchadnezzar for refusing to bow down to worship his image of gold. He gave them a final chance to change their minds, but they replied with amazing courage and confidence in their God:

> ...our God whom we serve is able to deliver us from the burning fiery furnace, and he will deliver us out of your hand, O king. But if not, be it known to you, O king, that we will not serve your gods or worship the golden image that you have set up.
>
> — DANIEL 3:17-18

They believed that God could save them, but they did not know if he would. Although they were unsure of his will, they were willing to 'let God be God' by continuing to trust and obey him, whatever the outcome.

This was how I felt. I believed that God could heal Megan, but I did not know if he would. I determined that it was my responsibility to cry out to him in faith, to plead with him for mercy, to believe that he could do the impossible. So for several times during this week, I found myself at my 'prayer square', pacing around that small grassy area, pouring my heart out to the Lord, acknowledging his sovereignty and mercy, his grace and wisdom. These were unique moments: I had never prayed like this before. If others noticed me, I did not care.

> In the days of his flesh, Jesus offered up prayers and supplications, with loud cries and tears, to him who was able to save him from death, and he was heard because of his reverence.

> — HEBREWS 5:7

As you may be facing the pressure and pain of life, here is a reminder of what Jesus felt and what he did while here on earth. His "loud cries and tears" in prayer to his heavenly Father remind us of how he suffered and how he coped. He understands how we feel.

7

PLEASE!

We were reconciled to staying in the hospital for several more days, but how long exactly, no-one could say. We brought in two duvets and a portable TV in an effort to make things more comfortable. On two occasions we went with our friends Wes and Karen to the self-service restaurant in the hospital hotel. It was a strange experience since many doctors, including consultants and staff who were caring for Megan would be eating in this same area. So many hospital personnel were there, taking a break from jobs that meant life or death for their patients, while we were there, taking a break from the strain of sitting at our daughter's side, fearing that she may never wake up. By now we were beginning to recognise other parents of sick children. The father of a teenage girl passed the time of day with me as we waited for the ward door to be unlocked. "How is she?" he asked. "In the balance," I replied. He explained how his daughter had gone through a similar experience as Megan a few weeks earlier. Like Megan, she had been fit and well one minute, and the next had needed to be rushed to hospital with a brain haemorrhage. Like Megan, she had been in intensive care for several days, following an operation. But now she was awake, speaking with her parents, even walking and smiling, though still not recovered fully. Here was hope for us in our desperate situation! Other children had recovered from Megan's condition! I dared to imagine Megan sitting up and talking with us, smiling at me. The longing became painful.

Then there was the visit from Caroline's uncle and aunt. Their daughter-in-law had been in a car crash about a year before. She had suffered brain injuries and had been in a coma, but was now making a good recovery. They knew, to a certain extent, how we were feeling and did their best to encourage us. Their parting words were memorable: 'The first squeeze of the hand is the most precious!' *Yes, Lord! Please let her squeeze my hand! Let her recognise my voice!* How I would reassure her that we loved her and were right there beside her! *Please, just some connection between us, some sign of life!* If this had happened to others, why not to us too?

But what was God's will? I knew enough from his Word to understand that it was not always his plan to heal, to deliver and restore, yet the Lord seemed to be giving us these encouragements from the experiences of others. Another amazing fact was that he was moving people from all over the world to pray for Megan. News filtered through to us from churches across America, Australia and the rest of Europe, as well as the UK. Christian people whom we had never met were praying for Megan and for us. Was this not the Lord at work? If he was going to take Megan from us, why all this intercession? I really wanted to believe that Megan would be restored. Did I lack faith? Or was it lack of courage, for fear of the desolation of dashed hopes? Or might it be God's purpose that Megan would die, and that he would be glorified, somehow, through the events that would follow her death? I just did not know, but gradually I developed a more positive outlook. I dared to hope.

Decision

Both our mothers had drawn strength from the Apostle Paul's words, when he speaks very honestly of his own suffering that had led him to despairing of life:

> We were under great pressure, far beyond our ability to endure, so that we despaired even of life. Indeed, in our hearts we felt the sentence of death. But this happened that we might not rely on ourselves but on God, who raises the dead. He has delivered us from

such a deadly peril, and he will deliver us. On him we
have set our hope that he will continue to deliver us,
as you help us by your prayers. Then many will give
thanks on our behalf for the gracious favour granted
us in answer to the prayers of many.

— 2 CORINTHIANS 1:8-11 NIV

The words fitted our perilous circumstances. They
recognized that as a family we were also under great
pressure, far beyond our ability to endure. And we were
being pushed towards relying on God for his help and
deliverance. We could gain confidence from the fact that
just as God had delivered Paul and his friends, so he
could deliver us from this terrible situation. There was
also the fact that many people were beginning to help us
through their prayers. And what would be the result of
all this?—the hope that many would "give thanks on our
behalf...in answer to the prayers of many" (vii). Surely
Megan's miraculous deliverance would result in great
praise and thanks being given to God for his gracious
favour? Of course it would!

This confidence found expression on the Wednesday
afternoon. Caroline had left to see the children again in
Southport. Mr. T, the anaesthetist, arranged for a private
meeting and several other staff accompanied him as we
gathered in the teenagers' room. He expressed concern
that I had no-one else with me, but I felt ready to receive

whatever news they would give. By this stage, Megan's condition had not shown any improvements, despite the best efforts of all the staff. Mr. B was present, the nurse on duty, and another anaesthetist, who did not seem quite as sensitive as the other staff. Mr. T was the spokesman. His words, always carefully chosen, were spoken calmly and sensitively. He explained that all the treatment they had attempted had not brought about any positive improvements in Megan's condition, which he had always depicted as serious from our very first meeting. The time had come to make a decision. Megan could be kept 'breathing' through the ventilator for days to come, and it was possible, with careful medical support, to maintain her current state for even weeks. But the time would come to bring Megan out of the induced coma to see if she could recover on her own. Perhaps that time had come. I felt the eyes of everyone upon me, gauging my response to this news. But their gazes were sympathetic, and I appreciated their sensitivity. Essentially Mr. T was suggesting that the process of removing the artificial means of sustaining Megan should begin. She was showing signs of 'multiple organ failure,' a phrase I will never forget.

I grasped what they were saying. I felt so vulnerable, yet at the same time I was conscious that I was a Christian and as far as I was aware, none of these people shared my faith. "So, what you are saying," I ventured, speaking for the first time, "is that we need a miracle."

After a brief pause the brash anaesthetist replied not so assertively, "Yes, but I'm afraid we don't specialise in miracles. We understand that you're in touch with Someone who does, but we are running out of therapeutic options." I did my best to remain dignified and thanked them sincerely for the excellent care they had given to Megan up till now. I cannot remember if I gave any consent to their suggestions at this stage, or even if I was asked to do so. What I do recall is that I had managed to confirm with them that should Megan recover it really would be a miracle, an act of God. I longed genuinely for two things: Megan's healing and God's glory. Did they need to be mutually exclusive? Mr. B spoke before our meeting closed. He had heard from a doctor friend in Leeds that people were praying for Megan even in his friend's church! By his own admission, this had impressed him. If this was so, what effects would Megan's recovery have upon him and the others?

8

DARKNESS

Thursday morning dawned. It was our tenth day in the hospital. Occasionally during this time I had glimpsed the relatives of other children, huddled in private rooms, their eyes red with tears. The hospital became a place of weeping and long, anxious exhalations of breath for so many. What would it be for us? Today something was going to happen. During these ten days many friends and family members had taken their turns of quiet vigil at Megan's side. It may have been on this morning that I returned from my 'prayer square' to find both grandfathers sitting at either side of her bed, praying silently. What was it costing these men, who had followed Christ for so many years, to see their precious granddaughter lying almost motionless before them? Would their intercessions prevail?

Both sets of parents returned to Southport, while

Wes and Karen remained with us. We took turns to sit with Megan. Wes spent some time reading aloud from one of her favourite books, *The Little White Horse*, the last book she had been reading but not managed to finish. Morning turned to afternoon, and the decision was made to move Megan to a smaller ward where the treatment and life-support machine would be removed. The four of us gathered around Megan and as the minutes ticked away each of us spoke to her. I assured her of my love and thanked her for all the joy she had given us. Caroline expressed how much she loved her, thanking her for being a lovely, precious daughter and such a great sister to Lloyd and Siân. The tears began to flow. Karen thanked her for being such a good friend to Catriona, their daughter. We prayed audibly and I committed Megan to the Lord who had given her to us. Everything became silent and still. The figures on the monitor displaying Megan's heartbeat decreased slowly, finally to nothing. "Oh! She's gone!" I heard Karen sob. Yes, it was true. We could stroke her hair, kiss her freckled forehead, caress her smooth cheeks, feel the warmth in her hands and arms, but she had gone.

I do not know how we continued from this point, how we spoke to the nurses, called our parents or gathered up our belongings from our room. What did it matter? Our daughter had died. In our own death-like trance we stumbled through these necessities, and drove back to our home, where Wes and Karen left us to return to their children. Lloyd and Siân had already gone to bed. The house was silent. On entering the front room, Caroline placed herself between her parents, I between mine, as though subconsciously we were regressing back to childhood. Our daughter's ten years of life had concluded abruptly with ten days in hospital. Hope had evaporated. Death had devastated us.

The next morning we gathered Lloyd and Siân into our bedroom and I prepared to break to them the news that their sister had died. *How do I do this? What words can I use to soften this blow that will wound them for a lifetime? How can I explain what I do not understand?* Looking into their faces I think they sensed what was coming. "Yesterday, the Lord decided to take Megan to heaven, to be with him," I began, hardly knowing what words to use. Siân asked a question or two about heaven, the typical response of a five-year-old seeking understanding. Lloyd said less. Then instinctively he left us, entered the bedroom he had shared with Megan, stretched himself out on her bed, covered his face and began to sob. Here was an eight-year-old boy expressing his loss. Was this his attempt to reach the sister he loved, who had always been there for him and with him, but was now beyond him? My heart broke at the scene. Did it have to be like this?

Ten years of life ended with ten days in hospital. A decade after her birth on that bright spring morning, the contrasts could not have been greater. Yes, once again I had been a helpless spectator beside a hospital bed, praying silent, fervent prayers, and willing digital figures to rise or fall. But this time there were no joyful celebrations. This time the doctors' faces remained taut and grey. There were no phone calls announcing happy news, and no joyful responses. This time nature's vibrant colours lost their lustre. The world turned grey and something died within me.

In the days of shock that followed I began to record and confront the grim reality in a notebook:

> I have to write this. Not so much for others to read but so that I will remember. On April 3, 2003 Megan, my ten-year-old daughter, died. At least, that is when her heart stopped beating. The events of this month have been more like a dream, a nightmare, from which I would love to awake. But each subsequent morning, and at certain still points through each day, I realise that what happened to Megan certainly took place.
>
> — April 16, 2003

But this was to be only the beginning of a long, painful road. We had entered "the valley of the shadow of death" and walked into the darkness. *How long, O Lord?*

Funeral

It hardly seems fair: almost as soon as a loved one dies, the bereaved face the responsibility of planning a funeral. Looking back it is difficult to explain how we found the energy and strength to do so, but I know for sure that God's help came to us through the practical support of our church family. Our first meeting with the funeral director was slightly surreal. He was a relatively young man, quietly spoken. I had liked his manner when I had met with him on several previous occasions as a pastor, to discuss the funeral plans for other people, usually old people, people belonging to our church or to local families. Now as parents we were discussing Megan's funeral: the plot where she would be buried, the type of coffin, and later, the clothes she would wear.

The funeral service was held at the Elim Pentecostal Church, since it could accommodate a larger gathering. We decided to hold a private burial service at the cemetery for family and close friends before moving onto the main, public service. We thought it best for Lloyd and Siân to remain at home for the burial, since they were so young and we feared the effects the experience might have upon them. In later years I have wondered about the wisdom of this decision. Would it have been better for them to witness the burial, despite their young years? I am still unsure. There are possibly no definite rights and wrongs when it comes to such decisions made in the midst of mourning. One has to make decisions at the time, and that is what we did.

Surrounded and supported by the rest of our loving family, Caroline and I laid our daughter to rest. The letters on the coffin recorded Megan's full name, and her age. I saw an official take out a white handkerchief to wipe his eyes as the coffin was carried to the grave. The hole in the earth seemed far too deep; the coffin far too small.

The church building was packed by the time we arrived from the cemetery. We discovered later that people had travelled from far and wide to be there. The head teacher had cancelled lessons and closed the school so that Megan's friends and other children, parents and teachers could attend the service. My colleague, Adam, gave a sensitive tribute to Megan, based on the various recollections of her friends from school and church. He likened her character to the fruits of the Spirit. Bill, a pastor from Liverpool, who had met and prayed with us in the hospital, sang his song: *My Days are in His Hands*, including a verse especially composed for Megan. Pastor Peter Day gave the address. The benediction was announced and we filed out from the front into the adjoining hall, where refreshments were provided and, more significantly, we would greet everyone. This was a time we had anticipated with some anxiety. How would we cope with meeting so many people? How could we manage their grief as well as try to handle our own? Amazingly we found ourselves carried along through this time, upheld by God's gracious Spirit, in answer to many prayers. The church family had pulled together to support us with prayer, love, sympathy and practical care.

One of the hymns we sang during the funeral service was *In Christ Alone*. The words are wonderful, expressing great confidence in Christ alone for our salvation and future hope, based securely on the death and resurrection of Jesus. The last verse is emphatic:

> No guilt in life, no fear in death—
> This is the pow'r of Christ in me;
> From life's first cry to final breath,
> Jesus commands my destiny.
> No pow'r of hell, no scheme
>   of man,
> Can ever pluck me from His hand;
> Till He returns or calls me home—
> Here in the pow'r of Christ I'll
>   stand.
>
> — TOWNEND AND GETTY, 2002

It is no wonder that the song is still a favourite today, chosen for weddings and baptisms, as well as funerals. Following Megan's funeral, however, it has been a bitter-sweet experience to sing it. We are transported back to those days and reminded of our loss. We recall Megan's *first cry* and *final breath.* The emotions are stirred again. But the truth remains the same: Megan was and is safe in Christ's hands; he called her home, and it is his power that we need continually to keep us standing in the days, months and years to come!

> How long, O LORD? Will you forget
> me for ever?
> How long will you hide your face
> from me?
> How long must I take counsel in
> my soul
> and have sorrow in my heart all
> the day?
>
> — PSALM 13:1-2

In times of deep sadness it can seem like you are alone—that God has forgotten you and that the sorrow you feel now will never go away. It can be a great comfort to know that others have felt like you feel, and have come through similar depths of sorrow. Psalm 13 is like that.

9

STRUGGLE

It was just over a month since Megan had died and we, as a family, were struggling to cope day by day. Soon after the funeral my parents had arranged a short holiday in France to help us rest. We were so grateful to a couple, originally from Wales, who owned a property near Carcassonne. We will never forget their tender welcome and warm hospitality. It was there that I started to write down my memories, thoughts and feelings. My first attempt at a poem was sparked by Lloyd coming into the house with a burst football.

> "Dad! Look what happened!"
> The new plastic ball—a present—
> was in his hands.
> But something was wrong.
> There was no bounce, little life.

"It fell among thorns" he
    explained, "but I've pulled
    them out!
What we need now, Dad, is
    Sellotape, and a pump!"
His eyes still had hope.
I squeezed the ball and felt the air
    exhaling from several places,
    against my lips.
I shook my head.
"Sellotape's not strong enough.
    That's it, I'm afraid."
His hands fell limp to his side.
His face fell. Hope evaporated.
No pump could keep that ball
    alive.
I felt like a doctor, imparting
    dreadful news to anxious
    parents
After hope has buoyed them up for
    several days.
There comes that hard but truthful
    moment
When words must state, however
    sensitively,
That no more can be done;
When disbelief must change
    places, and sad reality take its

    seat.
  "That ball was a fly away, Dad"—
    and it will fly no more.
  My daughter's flown away beyond
    my shore.

Our hosts planted a tree in Megan's honour in the grounds of their property, accompanied with a short inscription. That meant a great deal to us.

The holiday did us some good, but we were still emotionally exhausted as we returned home. Lloyd and Siân still needed our care and attention, and gave us the reason to get out of bed each morning. We stumbled into the month of May and while it was preferable not to go out and meet people, the Bank Holiday was an opportunity to get out of the house and take our children somewhere. Somewhere, that day, was the recently renovated Southport pier where we could at least walk, but it was quite a popular destination on that occasion.

We were just about coping with the crowds as we reached the end of the pier. Suddenly, we saw a face we recognised, a face from the hospital. It was the face of a father, whose daughter had been in the same unit as Megan; whose daughter had been seriously ill. He was the man I had spoken to briefly as we waited to be admitted to the ward. But there he was, along with his wife and his young daughter! She was walking with them, looking healthy and strong. They probably did not see us, but the sight of them brought all kinds of emotions to the surface. We should have been glad for them, but it was so hard not to feel the pain of our loss ever more acutely. We made as quick an exit as we could and walked home. Why, among all those people, had we seen that family? Why did she survive and not Megan? Why did we not have Megan walking down the pier with us, hand in hand, a family of five? It was a hard blow.

Later on, someone would describe incidents like this as grief's trip wires. You can be making your way through the day, perhaps just about coping, or better, with your mind occupied, when suddenly something will trigger your grief and you are transported back to square one of your pain and loss, like a cruel game of snakes and ladders! Those trip wires can take a variety of forms: a name, a flower, an aroma, a song.

10

ESCAPE

Now I can better understand why some people turn to alcohol or drugs; they are often running away from a reality too painful to bear. My experience of bereavement was so painful that I too longed to escape. Such longing can become so powerful that you are tempted to turn anywhere or try anything to find relief. Drink and drugs are the most obvious escape routes; there are others.

It made me think more than once of the poet John Keats. He had suffered the loss of his mother and then his brother, Tom, to tuberculosis. His own health was never strong. These lines from his "Ode to a Nightingale" capture his feelings. As he listens to the bird's beautiful song, he longs to drink some strong "vintage" and:

Fade far away, dissolve, and quite
    forget
What thou among the leaves hast
    never known,
The weariness, the fever, and
    the fret
Here, where men sit and hear each
    other groan;
Where palsy shakes a few, sad, last
    gray hairs,
Where youth grows pale, and
    spectre-thin, and dies;
Where but to think is to be full of
    sorrow
And leaden-eyed despairs,
Where Beauty cannot keep her
    lustrous eyes,
Or new Love pine at them beyond
    to-morrow.

Where could I find a shelter from this storm? I could identify readily with the urge to *fade far away, dissolve and quite forget*! Things that mattered once did not matter anymore. It felt as though I was being stalked by Grief, and I imagined him as an old man, dressed in a grubby raincoat. Like a private detective, he was constantly on my shoulder, watching my every move:

This old man Grief
Can't shake him off
I try to smile
He starts to cough

This old man Grief
Then drags me down
Converts my laugh
Into a frown

This old man Grief
Still shadows me
Though others squint
And cannot see

This old man Grief
So selfishly
Calls me away
From company

This old man Grief
Invades my space
He drives my car
He's in my face

This old man Grief!
This old man Grief!
When will I ever

Find relief?

Sometimes there is a welcome relief in the discovery that someone else knows how you feel. I found similar longings for escape from anguish expressed in the Bible. King David, long before Keats, expresses it so vividly, using the image of a dove:

> My heart is in anguish within me;
> the terrors of death have fallen
> upon me.
> Fear and trembling come upon me,
> and horror overwhelms me.
> And I say, "Oh, that I had wings
> like a dove!
> I would fly away and be at rest;
> yes, I would wander far away;
> I would lodge in the wilderness;
> Selah.
> I would hurry to find a shelter
> from the raging wind and
> tempest."

> — PSALM 55:4-8

It is worth pausing over some of these carefully chosen phrases: *anguish within me...terrors of death... fear and trembling...horror*. It seems that David wants us to appreciate how horrific his experience has been. Since this song was written I wonder how many people have read the lyrics and said, "Yes! That's exactly how I feel! I want to escape to my place of shelter!"? So what did David do? Did he fly or stand? Thankfully he tells us a little later: *Cast your burden on the* LORD, *and he will sustain you* (v22) and *But I will trust in you* (v23). David is not offering us a simplistic quick-fix to our storms of anguish. He has taken time to emphasise how horrific and overwhelming everything was for him. He is not making light of his horror. Out of his own experience he points us not to escapism, but to spiritual strength from a real and personal Lord. I am sure David wanted others not only to identify with his longing to fly away, but also with the reality of the Lord's sustaining power as we follow David's advice and cast our cares on him.

But how do we cast our cares on the Lord? It must be by turning regularly to him in prayer. It must involve admitting to him how we really feel. It must mean asking him for his strength to face life, rather than escape from it. I found these lines of a hymn, by Ellen E. Burman, to illustrate the kind of prayer I could offer:

> Teach me to live, 'tis easier far
>   to die,
> Gently and silently to pass away,
> On earth's long night to close the
>   heavy eye

And waken in the realms of
    glorious day.

Teach me that harder lesson, how
    to live,
To serve Thee in the darkest paths
    of life;
Arm me for conflict now, fresh
    vigour give
And make me more than
    conqueror in the strife.

11

ANGER

Do not go gentle into that good
     night,
Old age should burn and rave at
     close of day;
Rage, rage against the dying of the
     light.

Though wise men at their end
     know dark is right,
Because their words had forked no
     lightning they
Do not go gentle into that good
     night.

Good men, the last wave by, crying
     how bright

Their frail deeds might have
     danced in a green bay,
Rage, rage against the dying of the
     light.

Wild men who caught and sang
     the sun in flight,
And learn, too late, they grieved it
     on its way,
Do not go gentle into that good
     night.

Grave men, near death, who see
     with blinding sight
Blind eyes could blaze like meteors
     and be gay,
Rage, rage against the dying of the
     light.
And you, my father, there on the
     sad height,
Curse, bless, me now with your
     fierce tears, I pray.
Do not go gentle into that good
     night.
Rage, rage against the dying of the
     light.

In this, his most famous poem, Welsh poet Dylan

Thomas addresses men of all kinds—old, wise, good, wild and brave—as they face their day of death. There is a special poignancy in the last verse as Thomas addresses his own father. Perhaps the poem is an outburst of rage within Thomas against the brutal fact that his father will die. Is he right? Or should death be accepted quietly, submissively, naturally? Is there a place for rage? I do not think Dylan Thomas shared my Christian faith, yet I have some sympathy with his reaction.

We were bracing ourselves for our first Christmas without Megan and had decided to spend it in Cardiff, at the invitation of my brother. That first year of 'firsts' is the most painful—birthdays, holidays, Mother's Day, Father's Day—but Christmas is the worst. We were visiting some friends, Phil and Cathie. Phil sat with me in the car, parked in his drive, and talked. "What part of the day is worst?" he asked. I appreciated the question. It assumed that it was always bad, but some times were more acute than others. I had no mental energy to analyse this at the time; all I knew was that Megan's death had devastated us all as a family. Caroline and I were at a loss, stumbling individually through our grief and trying to support and understand each other. Lloyd and Siân did not know what to do. Megan had always been the catalyst for play and the mediator for peace. She had been amputated from us and the wound was gaping. Christmas was always a time of rejoicing and celebration, but not now for us or our wider family. Was this the time for stoic resignation? Were we meant to accept Megan's death as "just one of those things"? Or was there a place for anger?

I have felt angry—a rage mingled with grief and frustration. Sometimes it is irrational. I can remember being angry with the calendar, because it recorded those unwelcome and inescapable times and dates: a week since she died, a month since I saw her, a year since I heard her voice. I have felt anger again and again: when I found myself trying to comfort Caroline as she sobbed and groaned, but not knowing how, for all my words were spent; when we faced the misunderstandings of others and struggled with their responses to our loss; when I felt that fatherly instinct to protect and preserve my children, to put things right, and realised my failure; when I watched Caroline taking a baby wipe to clean Megan's cold grave stone with the same tender care with which she once washed Megan's warm face.

Time and again my imagination triggered the same scene: I would take a golf club (or sometimes an axe!), go out into our garden and vent my wrath by destroying the shed or hacking down the trees. I do not understand why this was. But always there was a strong desire to lash out and smash something, perhaps in retaliation to the way death had smashed us.

It may seem surprising to find individuals expressing their anger in the Bible. The prophet Jeremiah, sometimes known as the weeping prophet, penned many emotionally powerful words as he foresaw and foretold the spiritual 'death' of the nation of Judah. He lamented the rejection he faced from his own people because of the message he had been given from God. Sometimes it was too much to bear:

> Cursed be the day
> on which I was born!
> The day when my mother bore me,
> let it not be blessed!
> Cursed be the man who brought
> the news to my father,
> "A son is born to you,"
> making him very glad...
> Why did I come out from
> the womb
> to see toil and sorrow,
> and spend my days in shame?
>
> — JEREMIAH 20:14-15, 18

This is angry language; the language of grief. "Ah," someone might say, "this simply shows us that even Jeremiah the prophet was far from perfect. There were times when his faith failed, just like ours!" But is it as simple as that? Was the prophet wrong to express such feelings? Was this anger a lack of trust in God?

Job is another example. Many people remember him for the remarkable way he responded initially to the terrible news of the death of his children: *The LORD gave, and the LORD has taken away; blessed be the name of the LORD* (Job 1:21). But that is not all he said. After losing his health and sitting for a week among the ashes, scraping his skin with a piece of broken pottery, he blurts out:

> Let the day perish on which I was
>   born,
> and the night that said,
> 'A man is conceived.'
> Let that day be darkness!
> May God above not seek it,
> nor light shine upon it.
> Why is light given to him who is in
>   misery,
> and life to the bitter in soul…?
> For my sighing comes instead of
>   my bread,
> and my groanings are poured out
>   like water.
> For the thing that I fear comes
>   upon me,
> and what I dread befalls me.
> I am not at ease, nor am I quiet;
> I have no rest, but trouble comes.

This is not calm resignation—why are these words of Job not remembered so readily? Clearly, we can add Job to the angry list. Is there anyone else?

Something profound happened at Bethany, just two miles from Jerusalem, around 2,000 years ago. A family was in mourning. A young man, Lazarus, had died, leaving two sisters, Mary and Martha, to grieve. The whole town seemed to be mourning with them. Jesus, we are told in John's Gospel, had heard about Lazarus' sickness, but delayed his arrival for several days. We know that he loved this family and had stayed with them before. First Martha and then Mary greeted Jesus. They both expressed the same conviction: *Lord, if you had been here, our brother would not have died.* The narrative continues:

> When Jesus saw her weeping, and the Jews who had come with her also weeping, he was deeply moved in his spirit and greatly troubled. And he said, "Where have you laid him?" They said to him, "Lord, come and see." Jesus wept.
>
> — JOHN 11:33-35

I am struck by Jesus' reaction to the death of his

friend. He was *deeply moved*. Jesus, having arrived at the tomb, was again *deeply moved,* the same phrase. That does not sound like calm resignation to me. In fact, I understand that the Greek word, when applied to people, 'invariably suggests anger, outrage or emotional indignation' (*The Gospel According to John*, D A Carson, p415). The fact that Jesus, the Son of God, sheds tears of grief with and for those he loves, is remarkable. But something deeper is on display here at the grave. The Son of God is 'angry with the sin, sickness and death in this fallen world that wreaks so much havoc and generates so much sorrow' (D A Carson). Francis Schaeffer observes that in this scene Jesus was able to get angry with death without getting angry with himself. That means that I can also show anger against death without it being anger directed at God. This is an important distinction.

I am so grateful for Jesus' tears, but I am also grateful for his anger—not the anger of despair, since Jesus was about to raise Lazarus from the grave, but the strong emotional indignation at death's devastation. If Jesus himself joins others on the angry list then there must be a place for anger.

> If I could fight with Death
> If I could gain a hold
> I'd drag him down and kick and
>   punch

And leave him in the cold
For Death has caused me pain
And Death has pummelled me
Relentless punches still rain down
On all my family
But I cannot fight with Death
Just shadow box in vain
I lash out wildly in my grief
And miss, and miss again
To Easter I must look
To Christ, who fought for me
And won! So Death, where is your
    sting?
Where is your victory?
For all who trust in Christ
Will share his victory
One day we'll see the death of
    Death
And live eternally

12

LONGING

Break, break, break
On thy cold, grey stones, O sea
And I would that my words could
    utter
The thoughts that arise in me
And the stately ships go on
To their haven under the hill;
But O for the touch of a vanished
    hand,
And the sound of a voice that is
    still!

As a student, I wrote about this poem by Alfred Tennyson. He was affected deeply by the death of his best friend, Arthur Hallam, who died aged twenty-two. The grief he experienced, in a strange way, gave energy to his poetic expression. These lines came to mind as I longed just to see or hear or touch Megan again. I now knew all about such longing, intense and desperate; I ached for Megan to appear. Lloyd and Siân in time went back to school, and I would often be there in the playground to collect them at the end of the day. I longed to see Megan coming around the corner at school, among her class-mates, chatting away, just as before. That longing would weave its way into my dreams where she would appear with a smile and say, "Hi Dad!" And I would reply, "Megan! I love you! I've missed you! It's so good to have you back!" In the beauty of dreams no explanations are required; the joy of reunion eclipses every question and wipes away all tears. I would awake from these dreams with the dull ache of deep disappointment.

In the months and years following Megan's death, several elderly Christians from our church in Southport came to the end of their lives. In the days before they died I had the privilege of meeting with them and speaking to them, reading the Scriptures and reassuring them of the hope of being with Christ, which is far better. Several times I had a strong urge to ask them to take a message to Megan, to say that I missed her, that we loved her and longed to be with her! For the first time I understood why some bereaved relatives might visit a clairvoyant in a desperate effort to make contact with their loved one. We longed for a word, a voice, a message of reassurance that all was well.

This, of course, is part of the horror of death for those who remain. The practice of attempting to make contact with the dead has a long history. In the Old Testament it must have been part of Canaanite culture, because the Lord commands the Israelites not to consult mediums who practise such things. I concluded that it was wrong to try to speak directly to Megan, but there was something I could do with these longings. In the New Testament we are given glimpses into what happens to a person after death. For the Christian, the expectation is to be with Christ. I recall what Jesus said to the thief, hanging beside him, who cried out in faith: *"Jesus, remember me when you come into your kingdom." And he said to him, "Truly, I say to you, today you will be with me in Paradise"* (Luke 23:42-43). The Apostle Paul indicates his expectation of what happens at death when he says: *For to me to live is Christ, and to die is gain...My desire is to depart and be with Christ, for that is far better* (Philippians 1:21, 23). Again, Paul, speaking of the general hope of all Christians, writes of the preference to be away from the body and *at home with the Lord* (2 Corinthians 5:8). These verses assured me that, though we had buried Megan's body in a grave, her soul was now with Christ. Although I was not to seek direct communication with her, I could speak directly to the Lord in prayer. He is the Christian's great high priest, able to sympathise with my weaknesses. He had experienced grief and bereavement while here on earth. He could be the link between us. Could he convey my love and longings to Megan? How much could she know of our sadness over her loss? I am not certain. Some mysteries remain.

I believe that Megan is *Safely Home,* as we wrote on her gravestone; home in the immediate presence of the Lord she loved and trusted. I realised that for her to come back to earth and be with us again would mean loss for her. She is far better where she is. Yet for me, the longing remains.

> But O for the touch of a vanished
> 　　hand
> And the sound of a voice that is
> 　　still

What about the Prayers?

What about all the prayers that were offered up to God for Megan? Did they count for nothing? Could we have prayed harder? Did we not have enough faith? What about the promises in the Bible regarding prayer and faith?

Jesus told his disciples:

Truly, I say to you, whoever says to this mountain, 'Be taken up and thrown into the sea,' and does not doubt in his heart, but believes that what he says will come to pass, it will be done for him. Therefore I tell you, whatever you ask in prayer, believe that you have received it, and it will be yours.

— MARK 11:23-24

Whatever you ask in my name, this I will do, that the Father may be glorified in the Son. If you ask me for anything in my name, I will do it.

— JOHN 14:13-14

What was I to make of these promises? I was ready to admit that my prayers were often lacking bold assurance, but there were times when I really did believe that God could and would heal my daughter. I had even sketched out a sermon about the paralysed man who was brought by his friends to Jesus by letting him down through a hole in the roof. It says that *when Jesus saw their faith* he forgave the man's sins, and then healed him. My sermon points anticipated that Megan would be raised up by the power of Christ in response to similar faith and expectancy. I was ready to preach it in great triumph the following Sunday!

It was not just a question of my personal faith. What

about the faith of Caroline, our parents and relatives, and of so many other Christian people who had been praying so earnestly? Why had the Lord not responded to their faith? Had his promises failed? I knew deep down that such promises were not a blank cheque to believers to ask for just about anything—a sports car, a million pounds or a mansion! The Lord, unlike the genie in Aladdin, is not obliged to grant every wish. I had never regarded these promises in such a way. But on the other hand, I had not asked for material riches, just for my daughter to be healed. I had asked for this in his name.

I do not believe I can resolve this question fully, but I have found some help from a well-known passage in Paul's letters. The Apostle Paul—what a great man of faith! Surely God would listen to his requests? Surely Paul would ask with godly motives, in the name of Jesus? In his second letter to the Corinthians we read about a prayer he made to the Lord. It was all about this mysterious *thorn in the flesh, a messenger of Satan.* Commentators are not certain what this was exactly, and maybe that is just as well for us who read today. The interesting point is that Paul pleaded with the Lord three times to take this *thorn in the flesh* away. That sounds like serious, earnest prayer to me. But his prayer was not answered positively. The Lord did not grant Paul's request. Instead, he spoke to Paul: *"My grace is sufficient for you, for my power is made perfect in weakness."* So I concluded that it is possible for people to pray in the right way, with pure motives, with sufficient faith and urgency, and still not be granted their request. I realise that I must let God be God. The God and Father of our Lord Jesus Christ is also my heavenly Father. Good fathers reserve the right to say no to their children for good reasons. On the other hand, I knew that so many of the prayers made for us as a family were for God to sustain us, whatever the outcome. Such prayers had been answered. In our weakness, Christ's grace had been sufficient to keep us from despair, disbelief and divorce! But he had said no to the request for a miraculous recovery. I need God's grace to keep on accepting this, for it is far from easy. It is often difficult to see how Megan's death was for a good reason and even acceptance leads to further questions. The inescapable one is "Why?"

13

WHY?

"What have I done to deserve this?" This is often the question asked when things go wrong, and I could not help asking it myself in the aftermath of grief. Was Megan's death a punishment from God? Was he judging me for my sins? If I had been living an obedient, righteous life, pleasing to God, would Megan have died? How could I find answers to these questions?

My thoughts turned to King David's experience in the Bible. He committed adultery with Bathsheba, and she became pregnant. David, through orders sent to his general on the battlefield, proceeded to murder her husband and take Bathsheba as his wife. David thought his actions and schemes had gone undetected. Later, God sent the prophet Nathan to confront David with his sin. Part of the judgement David experienced was the death of the child Bathsheba had borne from their adulterous union (2 Samuel 12:14). Despite David's prayer and fasting, the child died. So here come the inevitable questions: "Was Megan's death a judgement for my sin? Had I done something that so displeased God that he saw it fit to strike Megan down?" I had to search my heart. It was quite possible to be tortured by such questions if I became convinced that I was to blame.

But there are other parts of the Bible to consider. I thought about Job, whom I have mentioned previously. He lost all ten children in one disaster when a strong wind destroyed the house in which they were feasting. His so-called friends insisted that Job must have sinned greatly against the Lord because, according to their theology of retribution, suffering is the automatic result of personal sin. However, the whole book of Job counteracts this view; we are told at the very beginning that Job is *blameless*. In fact, it is God who highlights Job's character: *he is blameless and upright, a man who fears God and shuns evil* (Job 1:8 NIV). The death of Job's children was not due to his personal wickedness. It was not a judgement from God, but it was a test of Job's faith. Satan had claimed that Job only feared God because God had blessed him materially. If the blessings of wealth and family were snatched away, then Job would curse God to his face. So God gave Satan permission to remove his riches, his flocks and family, to test the loyalty of Job's faith.

This passage raises all kinds of other questions, but it

highlighted for me one important point: the death of Job's children was not a judgement from God against his sin. So now I had David and Job to consider. Was my daughter's death a result of my sin or a test of my faith? Then I had to consider the Bible's teaching about God as the Christian's heavenly Father. One aspect of the Fatherhood of God is the fact that he disciplines his children. This is explored most clearly in Hebrews 12:1-13, where it is mentioned as a word of encouragement:

> My son, do not regard lightly the
>   discipline of the Lord,
> nor be weary when reproved
>   by him.
> For the Lord disciplines the one he
>   loves,
> and chastises every son whom he
>   receives.
>
> — HEBREWS 12:5-6

Today we think almost exclusively of discipline as punishment for wrong-doing. Admittedly, this is one aspect of discipline mentioned in the Old Testament proverb and repeated in Hebrews: *God punishes everyone he accepts as a son.* But I think the writer is trying to emphasise another perspective, the idea of discipline as training and development of character like the disciplined training a sports coach imposes on an athlete. This type of discipline comes through enduring trials and suffering. The Jewish believers to whom this letter is written had been suffering persecution for their faith in Christ. The writer reminds them of Jesus, God's perfect Son, who had endured such opposition from sinful men, and encourages them to consider him *so that you may not grow weary or fainthearted* (v3). He seems to be making a connection between the sufferings Jesus endured because of his faithfulness to God and the hardship they are facing due to their faithfulness to Christian.

It is for discipline that you have to endure. God is treating you as sons (v7). The writer seems to be saying that God, as their loving, perfect, heavenly Father, is allowing these hardships into their lives not because he is punishing them for their sins, but rather is perfecting their characters. In other words, hardship is for their long-term good. *For the moment all discipline seems painful rather than pleasant, but later it yields the peaceful fruit of righteousness to those who have been trained by it* (v11). So here was another possible response to the 'why?' question.

Another passage from the Gospels sheds further light on my questions. In John 9 Jesus' disciples come across a man who had been blind from birth. His disciples ask the inevitable question: *"Rabbi, who sinned, this man or his parents that he was born blind?"* (9:2) Their inquiry reveals a certain logic that must have flowed steadily down from the days of Job: 1) This man is suffering (he was born blind) 2) Suffering must be a consequence of personal sin 3) Therefore who sinned— this man or his parents?

Apparently, it was taught by some rabbis that babies in the womb could sin and therefore attract God's judgement! The disciples want to know. They do not ask, 'Why?' because they assume they already know the answer to that one: 'It's a punishment.' Instead they ask, 'Who?'—who was guilty? Did the man do something wrong before he was born? Or did one or both of his parents do something bad in God's sight so that God decided to inflict blindness upon their son as a punishment for them? I wonder if his parents, influenced by these religious explanations of the day, had lived with guilt every time they looked at their blind son.

I also wonder why the disciples ask this question. Were they interested in the theological debate? Were they asking from a purely theoretical position, or were some of them touched through personal family experience? I have no answer but it seems to me that as human beings, questions about suffering and guilt are never far away from us. They raise their heads frequently, either when we are confronted by a suffering world 'out there' or shattered by personal pain 'in here.' We seek explanations, we want answers.

Jesus' answer must have startled his disciples: *It was not that this man sinned, or his parents.* By this I think Jesus means not that they were sinless, but that none of the people concerned were being punished by this blindness for a specific sin. Jesus breaks the cast iron cause-and-effect logic of sin and suffering. He goes on to give his explanation: *but that the works of God might be displayed in him.* In this case the work of God was a work of grace. This poor man would be healed by Jesus' power and eventually came to personal faith in Jesus as he exclaims: *"Lord, I believe," and he worshipped him* (v38).

In his very helpful book, *When Heaven is Silent*, Ron Dunn tells how this passage helped him to come to terms with his son's tragic suicide. After months of frustration and soul-searching, he realised that, just like Jesus' disciples, he had been asking the wrong question. They asked the 'Who?' question; he was asking the "Why?" question. But Jesus was more interested in responding to another question:

> The right question, the one put forth by Christ Himself, is 'What now?' This question transforms the landscape of suffering from a random, accidental absurdity to a vital part of the grand scheme of a great God.

As a Christian, I had come to believe in the God of grace and I needed to come back to that grace again. I knew that by nature I had deliberately disobeyed God. I knew that by nature I deserved God's punishment, but I had discovered God's mercy and grace through Jesus Christ. Now I needed to remind myself of his grace to me through the good news which declares that when Christ died, he died for sins once for all. That means that his sacrifice on the cross was a full, sufficient, one-off payment for all my sins. The punishment that I deserved had been suffered already by Jesus, who gave himself for me. It was crucial for me to grasp this. My guilt had been atoned for. However, was Megan's death a test of our faith? Was this our heavenly Father's way of training us? Was there an unseen audience watching how we would react? I struggled to make sense of it all, but clearly the work of God in our case was not to heal our daughter. So 'What now?' I had to trust that the work of God would be displayed in our lives in another way. It was my turn to try to trust the Lord, and to believe the words of a song Megan had learned and sung at Sunday school: *God knows, God cares and he's working for good.*

14

SHARING

She lived unknown, and few
    could know
When Lucy ceased to be;
But she is in her grave, and Oh
The difference to me!

— WILLIAM WORDSWORTH

Whoever Lucy was, Wordsworth conveys his deep, personal sorrow following her death. It illustrates to me how grief is uniquely personal. When we hear of disasters in the news—a minibus crashes, killing children on a school trip; children are shot by a gunman on the rampage—Caroline and I now think almost immediately of the grieving parents. Although there is an overlap of grief linking us to them, we are very much aware that grief cannot be shared completely. It is intensely personal, and often isolating.

A few months after Megan's death, Caroline and I joined our church's 'Young Families' Weekend. In the past these events had been such great fun, with lots of children, games and activities. This time we had agreed to arrive just for the Saturday evening, and offered to share with our friends there how we were doing. There had been no opportunity to do this in the months up until then. Caroline and I chatted about what we should say as we drove across to the Quinta Centre in Shropshire. We had made a recent discovery. Some Christians in their grief felt the need to downplay the reality of suffering and emphasise the positives: God was good, his grace was sufficient, and they were pressing on in his strength. There had been a subtle pressure to be the same. What were we to say to our friends? Many of them and their children were still hurting deeply over Megan's loss. We decided to try to be honest. One of the leaders interviewed us. I recall one of his questions: "And how can we help you?" "Pray for us, that we'll have the strength just to get through each day. Most of the time I feel like curling up and dying." That is the truth about grief. Sharing this honestly turned out to be the best way for us and for our friends that night.

In May 2004, just over a year after Megan's death, we decided to attend a meeting especially for bereaved parents organised by *Care for the Family*. Trevor and Jo, a couple from our church, agreed to come too. Seven months after Megan's death, following a long period in hospital, Jo gave birth to Matthew, their first child. He was still-born, or as they subsequently chose to describe him on his grave stone, *born asleep*. Matthew was buried in the same cemetery as Megan, just a few plots away from her grave. I conducted a brief service as the small gathering of family and friends huddled around the grave and the tiny coffin was laid to rest. The insensitive wind swept across from the sea and buffeted us, as I read words from Psalm 42:7: *Deep calls to deep at the roar of your waterfalls; all your breakers and your waves have gone over me.*

That is exactly how it felt. Our church family was reeling from two huge breakers in the space of a few short months. Trevor and Jo supported each other. What did I know of their tragedy? I had not walked their painful path of empty arms and a silent cot. Their grief was unique, yet the chords of grief linked our hearts. And although conducting Matthew's funeral service was the last duty I wanted to fulfil, it seemed appropriate. I felt, in some way, qualified to read and speak and pray. Trevor and Jo felt this too, I think. We had all taken our place on the grieving bench, as Nicholas Wolterstorff describes it in his book, *Lament for a Son*.

So it was that on a bright Saturday morning in May we travelled across the Pennines together to a gathering for bereaved parents in Sheffield. We were anxious, of course. What format would it take? What might we be asked to do? The two guys, especially, had no desire to be embarrassed in any way! Was there still time to turn back and watch the Cup Final instead? On our arrival we were welcomed warmly and shown to our seats. The modern church hall had been arranged with around six sets of tables and chairs. Caroline and I were seated with a few other parents who had lost children of a similar age. Peter and Barbie Reynolds, the leaders, welcomed us again and introduced themselves. Peter introduced his wife as *the original Barbie*! They began by telling us their story of how, during one awful year of bereavement in their family, the final blow had been the loss of their son in a driving accident in South Africa. Suddenly I was aware that their words were triggering something in our hearts. It was not manipulated, but around the room I could just make out the sound of quiet weeping and a reaching for the box of tissues placed thoughtfully on each table. The emotion was not excessive, but real. The room was full of parents in pain, weeping out their sorrow. All our stories were unique and we would be given opportunities to tell them later, but we shared a common grief. We were not alone.

The day was especially helpful for two significant points I learned about grief. The first was made with the help of a visual aid: a ball, and three containers of differing sizes. Barbie explained that when our child dies our grief is overwhelming. Just as the ball was too large to fit into the smallest container, so our lives seem unable to hold our sorrow. As time passes, though our grief remains the same, our capacity to live and function enlarges ever so slightly, just as the same ball could just about fit into the second container. As she placed the same ball into the largest container, she emphasized that although we never 'get over' the loss of our child, we reach a stage when sufficient room can appear for other aspects of life to co-exist. We begin to find a 'new normal' for our lives. She warned us about the 'trip wires'; when something quite often innocent and always unexpected —a sound, sight or smell—can trigger off a new blast of grief. You are thrown back to earlier days of sorrow, sharp and severe. It was a great relief to hear someone describe grief like this as a result of their own experience. My sorrow over Megan's death was not something to be overcome and eventually left behind, but something that I could learn to live with.

The second help came when Peter and Barbie explained how they reacted to the death of their son, Simon. He shed tears, often uncontrollably; she hardly cried. He wanted to discover every detail surrounding the car accident; she only needed to be aware of the basic facts. There could not have been a greater contrast, but both were grieving in their own way. This was so helpful for us, since Caroline and I had shown similarly contrasting responses to the loss of Megan. Surprisingly, my experience was more like Barbie's, while Caroline's was similar to Peter's! This helped us to deal with a point of tension between us: why did I not cry like Caroline? Why was I unable to show more emotion? Did I not care as much as she did? Was I afraid to show my true feelings? Was I 'bottling it all up?' These were legitimate questions, but I was helped to see that we grieve uniquely, even though we share the same loss. People grieve in accordance with their personality. We know generally that some people 'wear their hearts on their sleeves.' Their emotions, whether joyful or sorrowful, are always near the surface. Others are less demonstrative; they show little and say less! Even good news is often confined to the privacy of their own hearts. Problems can arise when people are pressured or feel expected to grieve in ways that are not natural to their personalities.

We returned from that day thoroughly exhausted, but helpfully reassured. From all that we had learned our experiences and expressions of grief over Megan's death were quite natural. Our behaviour was not unusual, unnatural or even unspiritual. Above all, although our grief was intensely personal, we were comforted by the realisation that we were not alone. Like others, we would continue to grieve, and in doing so continue the struggle to find our new normal.

15

MYSTERY

The Bishop tells us: "When the
    boys come back
They will not be the same; for
    they'll have fought
In a just cause: they lead the last
    attack
On Anti-Christ; their comrades'
    blood has bought
New right to breed an honourable
    race,
They have challenged Death and
    dared him face to face."
"We're none of us the same!" the
    boys reply.
"For George lost both his legs; and
    Bill's stone blind;

Poor Jim's shot through the lungs
    and like to die,
And Bert's gone syphilitic; you'll
    not find
A chap who's served that hasn't
    found some change."
And the Bishop said: "The ways of
    God are strange!"

— SIEGFRIED SASSOON

I was studying A-level English literature when I first came across this war poem, entitled *They,* by Siegfried Sassoon. At the time I recall not being very impressed with either the Bishop's message or his response! The ways of God were strange because the young soldiers' horrific experiences did not fit in with the Bishop's grand and glorious portrayal of the First World War, but that final phrase, *the ways of God are strange,* which lodged in my mind for many years, now resurfaced. Was it ever right to say such a thing about God's ways? Was such an admission just a 'cop-out', a sign of spiritual or theological weakness? Is Christianity bankrupt when it comes to the really tough issues of suffering and tragedy? As an A-level student, I did not want shrugs and maybes, I wanted truth and certainty. There is such a strong human desire to have final answers and explanations. I am convinced that the explanations given to us in the

Bible—even to questions about suffering and grief—are the most convincing and persuasive, but does that mean that we will have an answer for every event or experience in life?

In Acts 12 we read about Peter's miraculous escape from prison. He has been arrested by Herod and is about to be executed, but the church is at work: *earnest prayer for him was made to God by the church* (v5). In response, an angel of the Lord appears and leads Peter out of his cell, past the guards, through the gates and into the open street. A miraculous deliverance indeed! So miraculous is it that when he turns up at the prayer meeting at Mary's house, the believers need some convincing that it is Peter and then, understandably, they are astonished. What a wonderful answer to prayer this was, and what an encouragement it must have been to the battered believers under Herod's cruel reign. In the excitement of the narrative we might just overlook the details at its beginning. Herod has already had James, the brother of John, put to death with the sword (v2).

Immediately my questions flow: Why did God not send an angel to deliver James? Did the church not pray fervently enough? Did God love Peter more than James? Would more glory have been given to God, and more encouragement given to the believers, if two Apostles had been rescued from Herod, not just one? From what I know about God from the rest of Scripture, he loved

Peter and James equally, and I find it difficult to imagine God saying to the Christians in Jerusalem, "If only you had prayed harder for James, I would have rescued him too." God's power was not limited; he could just as easily have rescued James. It does seem to me that God would have been glorified and the church encouraged all the more through the deliverance of both Peter and James. So, having addressed some of those questions, the original one remains: Why did God rescue Peter and not James? In the end I have to admit that I do not know the answer. It is a mystery—the mystery of God's providence.

After Megan's death I kept raising questions of my own and attempting to provide answers. Why had God not healed her miraculously? Surely that would have brought him greater glory. Maybe the Lord knew that Megan would face some terrible evil in this world, and so, to spare her from it, he took her to himself. But if God is sovereign, surely he could have delivered her in some other way? Did God have to resort to Megan's death in order to protect her? Maybe the Lord was going to use Megan's death to produce some radical change in our lives or the lives of others. But if he is almighty, could he not have chosen another way? Did it necessitate the death of our daughter? All these questions and counter-questions left me mentally exhausted!

The mysteries continue. The church prays for missionaries, but a young man dies in training while another fulfils years of fruitful service. Why? The church prays for its members, and the Lord preserves work for one, yet another faces the trauma and trials of unemployment. Why? Why is one lady healed while another faces life-long, chronic health problems? Why is one teenager saved in a car crash while another is killed instantly? Why is one sick child restored to her parents, yet another dies? At such times we must resist the strong temptation either to demand or to offer final explanations, for we may, like Job's 'friends', cause much more harm than good. At such times the wise and spiritually mature response is to acknowledge the mystery and say, "I just do not know why this has happened."

I believe in a God who is both sovereign and good, but he has not promised to give me all the answers here. I am still the creature; he is the Creator. There are times when I must keep learning to trust him 'in the dark'. We do well to admit it: there must be a place for mystery; sometimes *the ways of God are strange*.

> Why, O LORD, do you stand far
> away?
> Why do you hide yourself in times
> of trouble?
>
> — PSALM 10:1

It is interesting to see that many people in the Bible put questions like this to God. Perhaps you are asking similar questions at the moment. Life throws up scenarios which just do not make sense to us. It is not necessarily a sign of weakness or unbelief to ask God, "Why?"

16

MOURNING

It was Bonfire Night, another 'first' for us to endure in the year of 'firsts' following Megan's death. As usual, our church had arranged a bonfire event in a huge garden. As well as a massive bonfire there would be fireworks and music, soup and burgers, cakes and coffee. In the November darkness there seemed to be no end of people streaming into the venue. Children swarmed everywhere, wrapped up against the cold and chatting excitedly. It was the last place I wanted to be. A guest speaker had been invited to give a short gospel message. We greeted each other. It was the first time we had spoken since Megan's death. These occasions are not very easy for anyone. What do you say? He expressed his sympathy. I thanked him. Then he added, "But she knew the Lord..." and this was true. Megan had professed faith in Jesus Christ as her Saviour some time before. We have a wonderful record of her experience in her diary and it is very precious to us but it was not much of a comfort at that precise moment. The problem with such a response is that it seems to minimise death. My mind returned to the previous November, when we were a family of five, and all three children were wrapped up in their scarves and hats, filled with the excitement of the night. A year later, Caroline and I gazed up at the fireworks with a deep ache in our hearts. Megan's life had burned brightly for a while, illuminating many lives, but her sudden loss had plunged us into a darkness that we could hardly lift.

We discovered that some people, and especially Christian people, often felt the need to say something positive in order to help us feel better. I can fully understand why. To my regret, as a pastor I often had the same attitude: "What verse can I quote from the Bible that will make these folks feel better?" This is natural. If we really love people we do not like to see them hurting, we want to give comfort and relieve the pain. But when the pain is sharp and raw like an open wound, people can, with all good intentions, try to apply the plaster too quickly, too lightly. By contrast, a father at school came over to me soon after the funeral. He could hardly look at me. "I'm so sorry, Dyfan. I just don't know what to say..." That was all. He wandered away, probably feeling useless, but his response was so helpful. To me it was his attempt to acknowledge my devastation, which he could hardly imagine (his own daughter was in Megan's class). I was grateful for this.

The terrible year of 'firsts' was almost over when I attended a Christian conference in Leyland, Lancashire. I recognised hardly anyone and I was happy about that. Anonymity can be a welcome shelter. During a coffee break I bumped into someone I knew who expressed his sincere sympathy. As we walked through the church graveyard towards a seminar in the church hall I admitted, "Yes, it's been a very tough year for us..." "I'm sure it has," he replied, "and it will continue to be tough for a long time to come." Again, this was helpful. No plaster was applied; just an admission that the wound was deep and the healing would be slow. I remembered that this man had come through a long period of depression, and had written about it. He had admitted that he had had to revise his previous attitudes to depression and to those suffering with it—his first-hand experience had changed and perhaps mellowed him. It showed.

I am reminded again of Job's 'comforters' in the Bible. It strikes me that, in their case, the most comforting thing they did was to weep aloud and sit on the ground with him: *no one spoke a word to him, for they saw that his suffering was very great* (Job 2:13). The problems increased for Job when they began to sermonise, to try to rationalise and solve his situation. Their explanations were the last thing Job needed, and he refused to be comforted by them. We come across something similar, almost as a passing remark, in Matthew's Gospel. Through the Christmas narratives he records how King Herod slaughters all the children of Bethlehem up to the age of two in his attempts to destroy the one who was born king of the Jews. We can barely imagine the anguish of that town. Matthew adds this comment:

> Then was fulfilled what was
> spoken by the prophet
> Jeremiah:
> A voice was heard in Ramah,
> weeping and loud lamentation,
> Rachel weeping for her children;
> she refused to be comforted,
> because they are no more.
>
> — MATTHEW 2:17-18

It is that notion of refusing to be comforted that stands out. What kind of refusal might this be? I try to imagine the scene of grieving parents in Bethlehem. Do well-meaning members of the town try to hush them up or 'move them on' in their 'grieving process' so that they 'get over it?' Do some speak without thinking? "Well, you've still got your older kids." Do others offer spiritual counsel? "We must look forward to the resurrection." But the bereaved are hurt rather than helped. Like Rachel, they refuse to be comforted: "Don't try to comfort us like that! Don't try to fix us. If our weeping and great mourning is an embarrassment to you, then that's too bad! Our children are no more! Try to think about that! Weep with us. Pray for us. But don't try to push us into a state of 'feeling better'. That may make others feel ok, but we refuse that road to comfort. Our dear, dead children deserve better than that!"

Years after Megan's death I found words in *Lament for a Son*, by Nicholas Wolterstorff, to be a great help. His son died while climbing in the Alps. He acknowledges that people can sometimes say the wrong thing to bereaved people. He is sympathetic towards those who just do not know what to say. Then he adds:

But please: Don't say it's not really so bad. Because it is. Death is awful, demonic. If you think your task as comforter is to tell me really, all things considered, it's not so bad, you do not sit with me in my grief but place yourself off in the distance away from me. Over there, you are of no help. What I need to hear from you is that you recognise how painful it is. I need to hear from you that you are with me in my desperation. To comfort me, you have to come close. Come sit beside me on my mourning bench.

Of course, I am so grateful to God for the faith in Christ which Megan possessed. I draw great comfort from the prospect that one day we will be reunited. This is the hope of the gospel: *For since we believe that Jesus died and rose again, even so, through Jesus, God will bring with him those who have fallen asleep...and so we will always be with the Lord* (1 Thessalonians 4:14, 17). I am also grateful to God for the way he has cared for us through the steady, sensitive care of other people. In those early days people from our church family cooked meals, cleaned the house, and cared for Lloyd and Siân when we needed a break. Now there are those who tend Megan's grave in our absence, and still send us cards on her birthday and death-day. God has comforted us through so many of his people.

In Southport I knew an old man whose wife had died several years before. He had loved her dearly and missed her sorely. We once sat together at our kitchen table, drinking tea, as he reflected: "Some people say that time is a healer. It's not true. The Lord is the healer!" I agree. The Holy Spirit, the Comforter, knows just how and when to apply the healing ointment of the gospel to the wound of our souls. And as he does so, we know his comfort. The slow and gradual healing continues.

17

FUTILITY

At the end of our bed we keep a pine chest which is full of memories of Megan: photographs, diaries, school books, a school tie, drawings and letters. Two years after her death, on her birthday, I was re-visiting this special place. As I read her stories and admired her pictures, an overwhelming sense of futility washed over my soul. We had taught her to read, we had watched her grow, she had learned to tie her laces, write neatly (so neatly!) and play the flute. But what was it all for? She was snatched away by death after just ten years! What did it all mean? In the face of death everything seemed pointless. Why? Why? Why?! Why could she not have lived and gone on to use the gifts God had given her? She had so much to offer to the world! But this opened the door to another, larger question: If death, like a black hole in space, swallows up everyone in the end, what is the point of anything? Surely every effort, achievement and action is futile ultimately. Leo Tolstoy put it well when he asked: "Is there any meaning in my life that wouldn't be destroyed by the death that inevitably awaits me?"

Perhaps close encounters with death bring such questions into sharper focus. I remember a poem by Wilfred Owen, written during the First World War, entitled *Futility*. It describes a young soldier in the trenches who has just been killed. The voice of the poem, perhaps a fellow soldier, suggests moving him into the sun in the poignant hope that he might be revived. Then the questions flow:

> Are limbs so dear-achieved, are sides
> Full-nerved,—still warm,—too hard to stir?
> Was it for this the clay grew tall?
> O what made fatuous sunbeams toil
> To break earth's sleep at all?

Yes, that is how I felt. If life is going to end in death, what is the point of living? Why did the clay grow tall?

Then I remembered that the Bible asks this same question. Someone else had felt like this before me:

> Vanity of vanities, says the
>> Preacher,
> vanity of vanities! All is vanity.
> What does man gain by all the toil
> at which he toils under the sun?
> A generation goes, and a
>> generation comes,
> but the earth remains forever.

This teacher in Ecclesiastes is searching for meaning. He makes a shocking admission: *So I hated life...for all is vanity and a striving after wind* (2:17). This is his depressing but realistic conclusion about life in this world when he looks at it from an *under the sun* perspective, apart from God. This kind of cynicism is shared by many, and I was tempted to embrace it. However, as he allows himself eventually to view life with God in the frame, then the tone becomes more purposeful. This is how the book ends:

> The end of the matter; all has been heard. Fear God and keep his commandments, for this is the whole duty of man. For God will bring every deed into judgement, with every secret thing, whether good or evil.

> — ECCLESIASTES 12:13-14

This reference to God's judgement implies that death is not the end. It also infers, for that very reason, that life is significant; it has a purpose. When I was at school there was a huge difference between a subject that had an exam at the end of the year, and one that did not. Most pupils showed a very different attitude to the non-exam subjects, which often seemed pointless to them. This teacher concludes that life has an exam at the end, and that God is the examiner. In the light of this he does not seem to hate life anymore.

I am thankful for the author of Ecclesiastes, for the fact that God included this book in his Word. I am even more thankful that Ecclesiastes is not the only book in the Bible! When I turn to the clearer skies of the New Testament I discover that life is not swallowed up by death. I learn how God the Father has sent his Son into this world. Through his death and resurrection he has *abolished death and brought life and immortality to light through the gospel* (2 Timothy 1:10). The great news is that all his people, all those who have saving faith in Christ, will share in that victory. I hear the sure promise of resurrection and the hope of eternal life:

> For the trumpet will sound, and the dead will be raised imperishable, and we shall be changed...then shall come to pass the saying that is written:

> Death is swallowed up in victory.

O death, where is your victory?
O death, where is your sting?

The sting of death is sin, and the power of sin is the law. But thanks be to God, who gives us the victory through our Lord Jesus Christ.

— I CORINTHIANS 15:52, 54-56

It is this hope that has kept me sane and kept me going. It is this hope that delivers me from cynicism and despair, and makes every action and effort in this life significant and purposeful: *Therefore, my beloved brothers, be steadfast, immovable, always abounding in the work of the Lord, knowing that in the Lord your labour is not in vain* (I Corinthians 15:58). It is this hope that has sustained Christians throughout each generation, as one precious hymn, by William Gadsby, from the eighteenth century reveals:

> Immortal honours rest on
>   Jesus' head
> My God, my portion and my living
>   Bread
> In Him I live, upon Him cast
>   my care
> He saves from death, destruction
>   and despair.

18

HEAVEN

More recently I came across a poem by William Wordsworth, entitled *We Are Seven*. Its setting is near Conway, on the North Wales coast. Here is an extract:

> A simple child,
> That lightly draws its breath,
> And feels its life in every limb,
> What should it know of death?
>
> I met a little cottage Girl:
> She was eight years old, she said;
> Her hair was thick with many
>   a curl
> That clustered round her head.
>
> "Sisters and brothers, little Maid,

How many may you be?"
"How many? Seven in all," she said
And wondering looked at me.

"And where are they? I pray you
      tell."
She answered, "Seven are we;
And two of us at Conway dwell,
And two are gone to sea.

"Two of us in the church-yard lie,
My sister and my brother;
And, in the church-yard cottage, I
Dwell near them with my mother."

"How many are you, then," said I,
"If they two are in heaven?"
Quick was the little Maid's reply,
"O Master! we are seven."

"But they are dead; those two are
      dead!
Their spirits are in heaven!"
Twas throwing words away; for still
The little Maid would have her
      will,
And said, "Nay, we are seven!"

As bereaved parents we face this issue personally whenever we are asked, "And how many children do you have?" What do we say? It tends to depend upon the situation, but this simple conversation in the poem raises some profound questions. Is this simple child giving too simplistic an answer by insisting, in the present tense, *we are seven*? What about the voice of the poem's insistence that their spirits are in heaven? What does that mean?

Unlike me, Megan could draw! We treasure one of her pictures in particular—an A4 (landscape) of heaven! Jesus is centre-stage, sitting on a large throne, dressed in what looks rather like Joseph's technicolour dream-coat! In the background, placed symmetrically—two on either side of the throne—are four large hotels. In the foreground, on either side of the throne are two large angels, dressed in yellow, complete with wings and haloes. A red carpet flows forward from the throne, over which is placed a table of food, with plates of fish and chips, burgers, carrots and chicken. Large words capture the atmosphere: "HAPPINESS! JOY! ROOM! EVERYTHING!" The central notice at the bottom announces: "WELCOME—HEAVAN". The spelling mistake makes me smile.

Of course, some people would claim that the whole concept of heaven is a mistake. They might point out that Megan drew her own favourite food in her depiction of Paradise! They might argue that, in a similar way, people's belief in such a place is wishful thinking, a projection of our personal hopes and dreams, just happy thoughts of a place where people live happily ever after. They might add that heaven is a place 'somewhere over the rainbow' where, contrary to the famous song, dreams never really do come true. Perhaps they might concede that others can believe in heaven, if it helps them through this life, but they would scoff at any claim that it is an objective reality.

Following Megan's death we found ourselves re-examining so much of what we believed. Many Bible verses were now viewed from a new angle. One day Caroline asked me, "Do you ever wonder whether it's really true? I mean, is there really a place where Megan exists with God, a world we cannot see?" I confessed that I had been thinking through these matters too. Was it just a comforting concept to help us through the pain? Was Karl Marx right when he famously described religion as the 'opiate of the people'? After all, millions of people in the twentieth century were influenced by Marx's views. However, millions more, for twenty centuries, have listened to Jesus Christ. I thought I had better go back to the Gospels: did Jesus teach that heaven was a real place? Does life continue beyond the grave, or cease on the day you die? This is what I found.

From the beginning, his teaching was about the kingdom of heaven: *Repent, for the kingdom of heaven is at hand* (Matthew 4:17). He taught us to address God in prayer as: *Our Father in heaven* (Matthew 6:9). He warned about the false security of material possessions by contrasting the uncertainty of earthly treasures with the security of heaven:

> Do not lay up for yourselves treasures on earth, where moth and rust destroy and where thieves break in and steal, but lay up for yourselves treasures in heaven, where neither moth nor rust destroys and where thieves do not break in and steal. For where your treasure is, there your heart will be also.
>
> — MATTHEW 6:19-21

In one fascinating encounter with a young, rich, religious ruler, Jesus responds to his question: *"What must I do to inherit eternal life?"* What was interesting to me was the way Jesus interchanged the terms *eternal life*, *treasure in heaven* and entering *the kingdom of God* (Luke 18:22, 25). Then he presented his disciples with two realities: this present age and *the age to come* (v29-30). It seemed clear to me that when Jesus uses the terms eternal life, treasure in heaven and the age to come it is his way of describing a future objective reality.

The rest of the New Testament develops the picture by describing the reality of resurrection bodies for those who belong to Christ:

> But our citizenship is in heaven, and from it we await a

Saviour, the Lord Jesus Christ, who will transform our lowly body to be like his glorious body.

— PHILIPPIANS 3:20-21

There are also the glories of a renewed creation: *according to his promise we are waiting for new heavens and a new earth in which righteousness dwells* (2 Peter 3:13). The Christian hope for the future is therefore not some bodiless existence in a shining, other-worldly place far from Earth, but a physical, tangible, gloriously new Earth where we will hug and hold, climb and clap, singing the praises of our God and Saviour with undiluted and unhindered joy: *they shall obtain gladness and joy, and sorrow and sighing shall flee away* (Isaiah 35:10).

But what about the present? Where is heaven now? Does it exist? Peter, James and John once had the privilege of witnessing something remarkable. They accompanied Jesus up a high mountain and saw him transfigured before them: *His face shone like the sun, and his clothes became white as light* (Matthew 17: 2). Then they saw Moses and Elijah, talking with Jesus. I want to ask how they knew it was Moses and Elijah, but I am not told! This passage interests me because it shows the disciples seeing a reality that normally we do not see. Moses and Elijah were long dead! But here they are shown to be conscious contemporaries, aware of what is about to take place as Jesus heads to his death on the cross. Following Peter's suggestion of constructing three shelters, perhaps to prolong the experience, the disciples hear a supernatural voice from the bright enveloping cloud: *This is my beloved Son, with whom I am well pleased; listen to him* (Matthew 17:4-6). Some would like to dismiss this account as fictional. Others might wonder if we can be sure it happened. Many years later, Peter recalls his experience of this event and denies that it was just a scene from a fanciful concoction of *cleverly devised myths*:

> ...but we were eyewitnesses of his majesty. For when he received honour and glory from God the Father, and the voice was borne to him by the Majestic Glory, "This is my beloved Son, with whom I am well pleased," we ourselves heard this very voice borne from heaven, for we were with him on the holy mountain.
>
> — 2 PETER 1:16-18

Peter had witnessed something real that he would never forget: the sight and sound of the Majestic Glory; the sight and sound of a supernatural reality (and later was prepared to suffer and die in the hope of it). I appreciate what Francis Schaeffer had to say about this:

> According to the biblical view, there are two parts to

reality: the natural world—that which we see, normally; and the supernatural part. When we use the word "supernatural" however, we must be careful. The "supernatural" is really no more unusual in the universe, from the biblical viewpoint, than the natural. The only reason we call it the supernatural part is that usually we cannot see it. That is all. From a biblical view...reality has two halves, like two halves of an orange. You do not have the whole orange unless you have both parts. One part is normally seen, and the other is normally unseen.

— TRUE SPIRITUALITY, P63

To me it was becoming obvious that Jesus taught about this supernatural reality which he sometimes described as heaven. It is also true that Jesus, out of mercy and warning, taught about hell as the other part of the universe we do not normally see.

After Megan's death I could say with conviction: "We are five."

19

ITALY

> The LORD is my shepherd; I shall
> not want.
> He makes me lie down in
> green pastures.
> He leads me beside still waters.
> He restores my soul.

— PSALM 23:1-3

Is there life after death?—a question bereaved people are often forced to face. But there is another pressing question: Is there life after bereavement? How can life go on when the grief is so heavy? It seems almost impossible, unimaginable. In fact, you do not want life to go on. You want the world to stop! You cannot imagine ever being happy again.

In his book *When Heaven is Silent* Ron Dunn mentions how, several years after his son's suicide, a couple turned up at his church and were keen to speak with him at the end of the service. They thanked him for his sermon. 'It was nice to see you smile,' they commented. He had not heard that compliment before! But the couple soon explained its significance. They had recently lost a child and their pain was overwhelming. They wondered how they could continue. Then they heard that Pastor Dunn had also lost a son. So they had travelled to the church to listen and speak with him. The sight of his smile from the pulpit had given them hope. It showed them that life could possibly become more bearable; that some way down the road they might even find a place to smile.

As the first anniversary of Megan's death loomed, Caroline and I wondered what we should do, how we would cope. There was no script to follow. But God our heavenly Father had something planned. A few years earlier, a young mother had come along to the church toddler group. Gradually she became interested in the Christian faith, started coming along to church and eventually came to the point of receiving Jesus Christ as her Lord and Saviour. To our great joy as a church she was baptised. She was married to an Italian who came from near Turin (Torino). Not long afterwards they decided to return to Italy with their two young children. Now, after all that had happened to us, they invited us to visit them in Italy. We could be there over the anniversary of Megan's death. This proved to be a wonderful provision from God for us as a family, through the kindness of our friends. It also would lead to a new chapter in our lives.

It was our first ever visit to Italy, so everything was captivating! We stayed in Chieri, just outside Torino, a medieval town of ancient buildings and narrow roads, cobbled streets and quaint piazzas. Italian coffee and ice cream were simply sumptuous, and the city of Torino, with the snow-capped Alps in the background, was spectacular. So although the anniversary was painful— could it really be 12 months since we had last seen Megan? Held her hand? Heard her voice?—the experience of a new culture with the company of good friends, helped us through as a family.

We returned to Southport, where I had resumed my role in the church as co-pastor. My energy levels and emotional strength were significantly depleted, but I was managing to preach and function in a limited fashion. In many ways I found that the writing and delivery of a sermon was relatively easy; it was the interaction with lots of people at once that was draining. Now I felt that the Lord had lodged an interest in Italy in my heart, and not just because of the coffee! Caroline and I began to pray for the Lord to guide us. Through some remarkable 'coincidences' and conversations in the following months, we came into contact with the International

Church of Torino. The church had been praying for God to provide them with a pastor. Various discussions with the church leadership in Southport and correspondence with the leaders of the church in Torino took place. I became increasingly convinced that this was where God was calling us, but Caroline was less easily persuaded! Her mind, understandably, was taken up with the practicalities of where we would live, where the children would go to school and how we would cope with Italian! However, as time went on, all of us became excited at the prospect of the possibility of moving over to Italy.

Eventually, the International Church invited us to join them. A date was set for the move—April 2006, just after the Winter Olympics. The church family in Southport gave us a warm and emotional farewell. Through the Lord's provision of many loving, generous people who supported us financially and prayerfully, I was appointed as the International Church's first permanent pastor. We lived in Chieri, the charming medieval town where we had spent the first anniversary of Megan's death. Everything was new and exciting as it dawned on us that this was now our home. Through the International Church we met people from all over the world, baptised several new Christians, including Lloyd, and formed lasting friendships.

Living in Italy and pastoring an International Church had its unique pressures and frustrations. There were times when we felt completely out of our depth. But the

Lord proved to be faithful and sustained us by his grace. Through new friendships and experiences, the beauty of the Italian Alps, lakes and coastline, all within striking distance of Torino, we began to appreciate God's kindness and love towards us. Yes, we found that we also could not only smile but even laugh again!

> The LORD has done great things
>   for us;
> we are glad.
> Restore our fortunes, O Lord,
> like streams in the Negeb!
> Those who sow in tears
> shall reap with shouts of joy!
>
> — PSALM 126:3-5

I realise that for many people reading this chapter, who have *sown in tears*, the prospect of changing circumstances dramatically is out of the question. But I hope you can still find encouragement here. God holds out to you the hope of a measure of restoration, as David records of his experience of the Lord as his shepherd: *he restores my soul* (Psalm 23).

20

GLORY

There is a land of pure delight
Where saints immortal reign;
Infinite day excludes the night
And pleasures banish pain.

There everlasting spring abides,
And never-withering flowers;
Death, like a narrow sea, divides
This heavenly land from ours.

— Isaac Watts

When a book ends with the words "and they all lived happily ever after" we feel instinctively that it is a fairy tale, a fiction! We know that life in this world is just not like that. But what if there is a true story with a happy-ever-after ending?

Jesus promises it specifically to one man. In Luke 23, when Jesus is being crucified, almost everyone is hurling insults at him, including one of the criminals executed alongside him. Remarkably, the criminal on Christ's other side rebukes him. Then he turns to Jesus and, in an amazing expression of faith, makes his request: *"Jesus, remember me when you come into your kingdom."* To me, Jesus' reply is both wonderful and profound: *"Truly, I say to you, today you will be with me in Paradise."* Paradise? What could he mean? The word is Persian and means 'garden', but not just any old garden! The kings of Persia loved to create their own gardens of paradise. Years later I read more about this from the historian Tom Holland:

> Everything that [the king] could delight in, 'the beauty of the trees, the perfect accuracy with which they had been planted, the straightness of the lines they formed... the multitude of exquisite scents that mingled together and filled the air, had been ordered according to his pleasure.
>
> — Persian Fire p213 Tom Holland

That was the idea behind the word paradise! Jesus, as Christ or King, promises this nameless criminal, *"Truly, I say to you, today you will be with me in Paradise."* It is the paradise that Jesus has created; a place of pleasure and glory; a present reality for this man as he leaves this world, from unimaginable suffering to unimaginable joy. His body would, no doubt, be thrown aside—no dignified burial for him! But he would be with Christ in paradise!

Christians understand that Christ gives the same hope to all who trust in him. For me, that includes Megan, because she too, like the dying thief, had been drawn to simple faith in Christ.

But the Bible has another word to describe the hope that Christ came to give us: glory. We can read about it in a famous passage from the Apostle Paul, where he teaches about the Christian's experience of present suffering and future hope:

> I consider that our present sufferings are not worth comparing with the glory that will be revealed in us. For the creation waits in eager expectation for the children of God to be revealed. For the creation was subjected to frustration, not by its own choice, but by the will of the one who subjected it, in hope that the creation itself will be liberated from its bondage to decay and brought into the glorious freedom of the children of God. We know that the whole creation has been groaning as in the pains of childbirth right up to the present time. Not only so, but we ourselves, who have the firstfruits of the Spirit, groan inwardly as we

wait eagerly for our adoption as sons, the redemption of our bodies. For in this hope we were saved. But hope that is seen is no hope at all. Who hopes for what he already has? But if we hope for what we do not yet have, we wait for it patiently.

— ROMANS 8:18-25 NIV

Notice that Paul pictures *creation groaning,* longing for a kind of re-birth, when it will be *liberated from its bondage to decay.* He describes Christians groaning *inwardly* as we wait eagerly for *the redemption of our bodies.* He has the resurrection in mind, which will take place when Jesus Christ returns to make all things new —transforming this earth into his glorious paradise, heaven on earth!

He will wipe away every tear from their eyes, and death shall be no more, neither shall there be mourning, nor crying, nor pain any more, for the former things have passed away.

— REVELATION 21:4

The question remains: Is it true? Or is it just a fairy tale?

I am left with a decision to make, a question to answer. It is a question that, in effect, rises above every other: will I trust Jesus Christ? Do I believe what he says? Or will I turn away? What about you?

I think back to a scene where Jesus has been teaching the crowds about himself and the need to respond to him. He has made some exclusive claims: *And this is the will of him who sent me, that I should lose nothing of all that he has given me, but raise it up on the last day* (John 6:39-40). Many people in the crowd cannot stomach this anymore: *After this many of his disciples turned back and no longer walked with him* (v66). This is also the real temptation that many Christians face in the middle of sufferings and trials. "Is it really true?" we wonder. "Is it worth believing anymore?" Perhaps you are reading this book because you are at that point now.

Jesus turns to his twelve disciples and asks: *"Do you want to go away as well?"* And Peter, despite all his faults, doubts and fears, replies:

> Lord, to whom shall we go? You have the words of eternal life, and we have believed, and have come to know, that you are the Holy One of God.
>
> — JOHN 6:68-69

I feel like Peter. Despite my grief, anger, longings and unanswered questions, I find myself drawn back to Jesus Christ and saying, "Lord, there is nowhere else to go. You have the words of eternal life, and you alone offer the hope of eternal life. You went through unimaginable suffering to pay for my sins, so that I might enjoy unimaginable glory with you forever. You have conquered death and live forever. Help me to keep trusting you. Help us—Caroline and me, Lloyd and Siân —to keep looking to you. And you will raise us up on the last day, along with Megan, and all those who have believed in you, according to your promise."

Like the sunflowers in France, all those years ago, we will continue to look "east", as it were, to the return of the Son and the glorious promise of resurrection, re-creation and reunion in him. My prayer is that this book will encourage you to do the same—to look to Jesus Christ as your only hope and comfort. And if you have done so, my prayer is that you continue to call upon him and trust him, whatever you have been through.

But there is another image—travelling on the journey of faith with the certain expectation of home, the hope of glory. Each day, no matter how painful the path may be, the Christian is getting nearer home, when eventually, *the traveller's journey is done* (William Blake). I would like to give the last word to John Bunyan, who expressed the longing and hope of glory so vividly towards his conclusion of *Pilgrim's Progress,* with imagery borrowed from the book of Revelation:

Now I saw in my dream, that these two men [Christian and Hopeful] went in at the Gate; and lo, as they entered they were transfigured, and they had raiment put on that shone like gold. There was also that met them, with harps and crowns, and gave them to them, the harp to praise withal, and the crowns in token of honour. Then I heard in my dream, that all the bells in the City rang again for joy; and that it was said unto them, "ENTER YE INTO THE JOY OF YOUR LORD." I also heard the men themselves, that they sang with a loud voice, saying, "BLESSING, HONOUR, GLORY, AND POWER, BE TO HIM THAT SITTETH UPON THE THRONE AND TO THE LAMB FOR EVER AND EVER."

Now just as the gates were opened to let in the men, I looked in after them; and behold, the City shone like the sun, the streets also were paved with gold, and in them walked many men with crowns on their heads, palms in their hands, and golden harps to sing praises withal.

There were also of them that had wings, and they answered one another without intermission, saying, "HOLY, HOLY, HOLY, IS THE LORD". And after that, they shut up the gates: which when I had seen, I wished myself among them.